Financial Control
for Non-financial
Managers

Financial Control for Non-financial Managers

.

DAVID IRWIN

the Institute
of Management

F O U N D A T I O N

PITMAN
PUBLISHING

PITMAN PUBLISHING
128 Long Acre, London WC2E 9AN

A Division of Pearson Professional Limited

First published in Great Britain 1995

© David Irwin 1995

British Library Cataloguing in Publication Data
A CIP catalogue record for this book can be obtained
from the British Library

ISBN 0 273 61972 1

1 3 5 7 9 10 8 6 4 2

Transferred to digital print on demand, 2002
Printed & Bound by Antony Rowe Ltd, Eastbourne

*The Publishers' policy is to use paper manufactured
from sustainable forests.*

Contents

■

Preface   vii

Acknowledgements   ix

PART 1: NEED FOR FINANCIAL CONTROL

1 **Is your business profitable?**   3

2 **Business objectives**   14

PART 2: UNDERSTANDING THE FIGURES

3 **Financial statements**   29

4 **Interpreting accounts**   47

PART 3: PLANNING FOR PROFIT

5 **Costing and pricing**   71

6 **Planning capital assets**   89

7 **Formulating the plan**   105

PART 4: EXERCISING CONTROL

8 **Collecting the information**   125

9 **Keeping track of the figures**   153

10 **Using the figures**   174

Glossary   183

Further reading   187

Answers to the exercises   188

Preface

■

This book is intended to assist managers who have a financial responsibility but not an accounting background. It will be particularly helpful to managers who are not in a position easily to call on the 'company accountant'. The typical reader will have, nevertheless, some responsibility for financial planning and financial control. This might include, for example, owner managers of small businesses employing, perhaps, up to 25 staff; managers within smaller businesses; and managers of departments in larger businesses or other organisations.

The book follows a logical progression from demonstrating the need for effective control and understanding financial statements, through preparing business objectives and budgets to collecting appropriate information and using that information to identify when corrective action needs to be taken. In other words, this book focuses on how you as a manager or entrepreneur can understand and use the figures at your disposal to control the business in which you work.

It may be worth a brief word about what the book does not set out to cover. It does not aim to suggest ways of introducing controls to ensure invoices are sent out correctly or that stock is checked in correctly or that there is no fraud. Controls such as these are certainly needed, possibly backed up by occasional (or for larger businesses, regular) internal audit arrangements. Companies will also require annual external audits. These will, to a large extent, ensure that proper controls are in place. In some larger organisations, particularly the NHS for example, audits are intended to ensure that they are performing 'economically, efficiently and effectively'. External auditors also need to satisfy themselves that businesses are unlikely to become insolvent at least in the immediate future. But external audit is really about demonstrating accountability to shareholders and other stakeholders. It will not help in ensuring those three Es are achieved on a daily basis.

On the other hand if you prepare management accounts on a regular basis, and if you understand what the figures tell you, then you will be able to retain effective financial control. I have set out to emphasise the importance of this and to suggest ways in which objectives can be set and the figures monitored to identify whether the business or organisation is on target or whether corrective action needs to be taken. To achieve that objective it is necessary to devote one chapter to understanding financial statements and one to book-keeping. It is not intended, however, to teach book-keeping. If you require a greater understanding of book-keeping, then you should refer to one of the many books devoted to that subject.

Most benefit will be derived from reading the entire book, but those of you who already have some knowledge may choose to disregard certain chapters without detracting from the rest of the book.

David Irwin
May 1995

Acknowledgements

■

I am very grateful to all my clients, named or otherwise, who have inspired the examples and case studies used throughout this book. Particular thanks are due to

- Young & Co's Brewery plc for permission to use figures from their 1994 annual accounts. As well as providing all the statutory figures, Young & Co aim in their annual report to give a very simple explanation of their accounts which is understandable by anyone.
- Sage Group plc for permission to include examples from their computerised accounting packages.
- Centre for Interfirm Companies for permission to use illustrations from their marketing materials.
- Midland Bank for preparing a facsimile bank statement.

I would like to thank Ian Laybourn, Alan le Marinel, Sandy Ogilvie, John Oswald, Gordon Kinghorn and Hew Irwin for reading the draft and for their helpful comments and also Roy Gaylor, who did a marvellous editing job correcting poor grammar and spotting numerical mistakes. I am particularly grateful to Ian Thompson who acted as a sounding board for many of the ideas, who was extremely helpful in ensuring that the chapter on book-keeping is understandable and who checked all my arithmetic. Any mistakes remaining are, however, my responsibility. Thank you to Tracy Gee, Pat Heywood, Kymm Robinson, Fiona Landells and Amanda Compton for their assistance in typing innumerable drafts and Sonya Rooke for preparing the illustrations.

I am extremely grateful to my wife Jane for allowing me to have the peace and quiet necessary to complete this book and for her love and encouragement throughout.

Part 1

■

Need for financial control

1

Is your business profitable?

■ It is essential for every business to make a profit, otherwise it will
  not stay in business for long.

■ It is necessary to have a plan and to monitor actual performance
  against that plan in order to ensure that the business is profitable.

■ Effective financial control can be achieved by monitoring a
  relatively small number of figures and identifying variations that
  require attention.

Introduction

If you are managing a department or division in a business, running
your own business or managing a charitable organisation, you will
know how much courage, commitment and hard work is required to
succeed and prosper. Success and prosperity requires successful marketing, successful financial control and success in managing and moti-
vating your staff. Many people move into management because they
are good 'at what they do', but they are not necessarily equipped at the
outset to be competent in everything that managers have to do. In
small organisations, in particular, there is an expectation that managers can do everything. In small businesses such tasks usually fall to
the proprietor. For many managers, and for many entrepreneurs, exercising effective financial control is, at best, seen as a mystery and, at
worst, not even considered. Yet monitoring a small number of important figures can ensure that you retain complete and effective financial
control. This should ensure that the business stays profitable; it will
certainly ensure that you are able to live within agreed borrowing
facilities and that you are in a position to take corrective action before
it is too late.

We live in a changing world, arguably the change we face has never
been so great. Technology advances with dramatic rapidity – twenty

years ago forecasters told us that the fax, video recorder and personal computer would have little effect. The Walkman was not yet a gleam in Sony's eye. Economic change is similarly dramatic. The single European market has cut trade barriers and exposed more businesses to more competition, as well as to more opportunities. The fall of communist regimes in the countries of central and eastern Europe and their desire to join the European Community will ensure change continues. Their lower labour rates will also have an effect as more businesses sub-contract, or move completely, to those countries. The developing world, too, boasts low labour costs. The increasing power of computers and improving communications makes it very easy, especially for knowledge based industries, to undertake work where labour costs are lowest.

The government, too, impinges on businesses' costs – indirectly through interest rates, inflation and exchange rates – and directly through, for example, health and safety legislation, environmental legislation and changes in national insurance arrangements. Most recently, their power to affect costs has been seen with the introduction of new taxes on insurance and air travel.

4

In a world like this, managers and entrepreneurs have to concentrate their efforts on their strategy and on their marketing. Those businesses which have an effective system of financial control will have more time available to worry about their marketing and more information to assist in developing their strategy.

This book is intended to help you put in place that financial control: to ensure that you are making a profit, to ensure that you are estimating costs accurately and then keeping them under control, to ensure that you are charging the right price and to ensure that you can collect money owed to you and can pay your debts as they fall due. Financial control is different to book-keeping. Book-keeping is about recording the figures: income and expenditure; receipts and payments; assets and liabilities. Accurate book-keeping, of course, is a prerequisite for effective financial control and computerised accounting packages such as those from Sage Group plc, make accurate book-keeping very easy.

The objectives of this book are

- to demonstrate how effective financial control assists in the management of the organisation in which you work;
- to show how that control can be achieved through simple documentation; and,
- to suggest appropriate financial indicators for inclusion in your strategic objectives.

All businesses experience problems. Some of these problems are beyond your control, such as interest rates or the latest consumer fad. Many problems, however, need not arise if care is taken to ensure that you understand what is happening at all times. Look at how many businesses, apparently successful, have suddenly failed. Wildly exceeding your sales forecast can cause cash flow problems as severe as failing to reach the forecast. By the end of this chapter, you should understand which are the most important aspects of your business over which to exercise control and, in particular, appreciate the importance of good financial control.

The importance of making a profit

The objective of every commercial business is to make a profit. Without a profit you cannot reward the investors for their stake in the business (including yourself if you are the sole investor), nor will you have enough money for reinvestment to make the business grow. And that profit has to come after paying all the staff as well as all the other expenses. To do that you need a product or service that is marketable and which you can persuade customers to buy at a price in excess of the costs. For most businesses, prices tend to be market based so costs must be controlled to keep sufficiently below the price in order to make a profit.

Large companies generally aim to maximise their profits over the long term. This increases shareholder value and gives the investors a regular dividend. Private companies do not need to worry about profit maximisation if they choose not to. They are not vulnerable to takeovers and the shareholders may have other objectives. Working shareholders, sole proprietors or partners may agree, for example, to forego some of the potential profit because they prefer to work less hard. One of the great benefits of working for oneself is the opportunity to do work that is fun and rewarding. Of course, there will be tasks, as with any job, that may seem tedious and time-consuming, but overall I believe that owner managers should be seeking a balance between fun and reward. However, if they do not aim for a realistic profit, there is always the danger that they will make a loss and businesses which continually lose money quickly cease to trade.

If you have invested money in the business, is the reward greater than the *opportunity cost*? For example, if you have £20,000 available you might receive interest of 10 per cent every year (after tax) from the bank or building society. If you use that money for your business instead, then you need to generate a return better than 10 per cent.

5

The opportunity cost is the income foregone by not choosing a specific opportunity. In this case it is £2,000 per annum (i.e. 10% x 20,000). If you cannot do at least this well, you might decide that you would be better off working for someone else and reinvesting your money elsewhere. Similarly, if you need to borrow money from the bank, you need to ensure that you are generating a return that is considerably greater than the interest that you have to pay the bank, otherwise you end up working for the bank instead of yourself.

Many people do not think carefully enough about the cost of borrowing money, only looking at the size of the monthly repayments. But cost is an important consideration. Later, we will look at ways of assessing the cost of loan finance relative to the profit of the business. Naturally, there will be occasions when you need to borrow large sums of money, perhaps for short periods. This will be far easier if your business is profitable and if you can demonstrate to potential lenders, such as the banks, that you are in control and know the exact financial position of the business.

Making a profit is just as important in the so-called not-for-profit organisation. The feature which distinguishes not-for-profit organisations is that they do not have shareholders and do not, therefore, distribute the profit. Instead, all profit is retained and ploughed back into the work of the organisation. While the key objective for such organisations will not be a financial one, they need to take exactly the same care as any other business to ensure that their costs are under control and that they do not make a loss.

It is not enough, however, for businesses simply to aim to make a profit. If they do, they are likely to hop from one opportunity to another. The most successful businesses are usually driven by a clear sense of purpose and by core values shared widely by the staff.

What are the key activities for success?

There are four major aspects of running a business which need particular care if the business is to be successful. First, the business has to be able to provide a product or service efficiently, of the right quality, at an acceptable cost and at the right time.

Second, the product or service must be effectively marketed to the prospective customer. The customer must be prepared to pay more for the benefits that they derive than it costs you to provide the features. The difference between cost and price is your profit. We will be looking at the relationship between cost and price in some detail later. It is important to satisfy the needs of your customers. When asked what his business did, Charles Revlon, founder of Revlon, replied: 'In the factory we make cosmetics; in the store we sell hope'. In other words, businesses sell *features*, but people buy *benefits*. This is true of every product or service.

Features are what a product has or is, e.g. size, colour, attachments, etc. Benefits are what the product does for the customer. It is important to understand the features that you are providing but it is equally important to be clear about, and to communicate, the benefits that you are offering your customers.

Consider this statement: This hi-fi amplifier has a frequency response of 30Hz to 20kHz $\pm$ 1½ dB, a power output of 35 watts RMS per channel and cross talk between channels better than -45 dB. Most potential customers would be totally bamboozled. What they want to know is that there will be no noticeable distortion over the range of human hearing at a volume loud enough to fill an average sitting room.

Let's look at a further example which demonstrates how the features of an automatic camera provide benefits to the user:

7

EXAMPLE

Feature/benefit analysis: camera

Feature	Benefit
■ Autofocus lens-shutter and active autofocus system	■ Focuses automatically to provide instant response to catch that magic moment
■ Programmed electronic shutter	■ Sets shutter automatically to provide that instant response
■ Uses 35mm standard DX coded film	■ Sets film speed automatically
■ 35mm F3.5 lens	■ Wide angle lens maximising field of view
■ Self timer	■ Enables photographer to be in own picture

Third, you need to exercise tight financial control. It is extremely easy for the costs to run away, to waste materials and to sell products or services too cheaply. At best, this will reduce profit; at worst, the business will make a loss and, eventually, fail.

Finally, you need to be aware of the business's human resource needs. Once a business starts to employ people you will have to think about recruitment, induction, career development, training, motivation, etc. This all costs extra money, but should be regarded as an investment in exactly the same way as you might expect to invest in machinery. The business depends on the people employed, so treat them properly. Running a business, or a unit within a business, means that you are continually faced with a series of events for which decisions have to be taken. The right decisions depend upon having the right information easily available. This is as true for information about the business's financial position as for every other aspect of running the business.

The working capital cycle

Clearly, you cannot simply spend, spend, spend unless there is sufficient money coming into the business to cover the expenditure, or unless arrangements have been made for finance to cover that expenditure. In the production process a business takes raw materials; it *adds value* by turning those materials into a saleable product; and then it sells and dispatches the product to a customer. At each stage it may have stocks of raw materials or of work in progress or of finished goods (see Figure 1.1)

Following the cash is often more complicated than following the products! You may not pay immediately for what you buy. You will need to ensure that you have sufficient funds available to cover your stock, which includes raw materials, work in progress and finished goods. (Even if you are a service-based business you may well hold raw materials or have what is effectively work in progress.) Once you deliver those goods (or services) to your customer then you have sold them. But you may not be paid for some time. The eventual payment releases cash which can be used to pay your suppliers, to pay the fixed costs and to provide a profit. The money tied up in this way is known as working capital.

Usually it is relatively straightforward to take decisions about capital expenditure. You can assess the need for a piece of equipment or a new vehicle; you can see what it will cost and know whether you have or can borrow the money. It becomes more difficult if you need more than one item but cannot afford everything, although there are techniques to help you choose.

It is considerably more difficult, however, to control working capital. Sometimes businesses discover that there is considerable demand for their product. They buy more stock, make more goods, sell more products – all apparently at a profit. Then they discover that their customers do not pay soon enough but their suppliers are demanding payment. In other words, their working capital requirement has grown, but their actual growth in working capital has failed to keep pace with their growth in sales. This is known as over-trading.

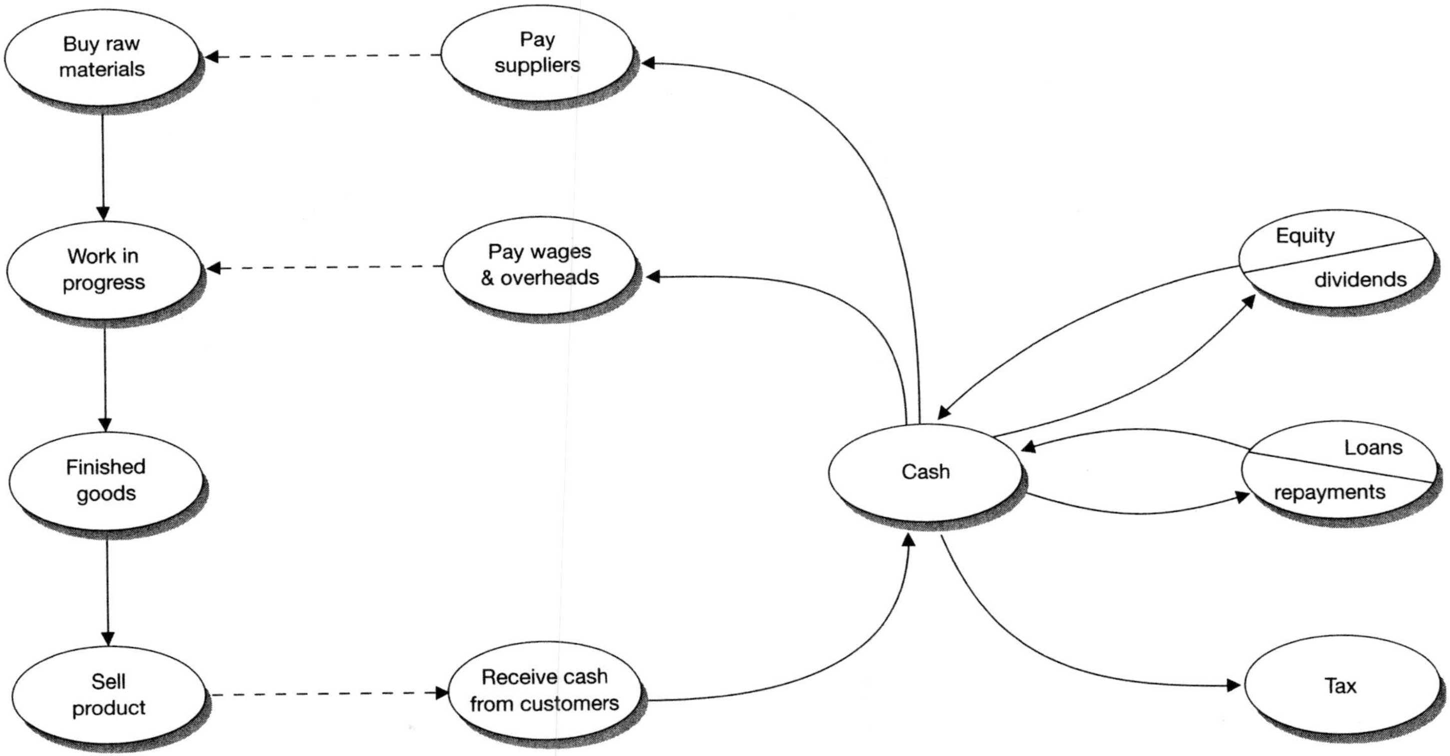

9

Figure 1.1 Working capital cycle

A business is solvent if it has sufficient assets (cash, stock, debtors, fixed assets) to cover its liabilities (loans, creditors, etc.). However, a business also has to be able to meet debts as they fall due. If it doesn't have sufficient cash, or sufficient assets that can quickly be turned into cash (often known as liquid assets), then it may be regarded as insolvent. Trading when knowingly insolvent is now an offence, so care must be taken. Sole traders and partnerships have always had unlimited liability: that means that they are personally liable for all debts incurred by the business. Companies normally have limited liability: the shareholders will lose only their investment if the business fails. However, if it can be demonstrated that the directors knew a company was trading whilst insolvent, then they can be held to be personally liable.

If sales are relatively stable, and if collection and payment periods are stable, there will be an equilibrium between current assets and current liabilities. If customers suddenly pay more slowly, or suppliers suddenly demand faster payment, or sales start to increase, then the business will require an increase in working capital. Businesses can sometimes use their retained earnings to provide this additional working capital requirement but, if that is insufficient, the overdraft facility may need to be increased. Preparing cash flow forecasts, comparing performance against forecast, and regularly updating the forecast will assist in managing your working capital.

You will need to think carefully about all these needs and incorporate them, together with your sales forecast, into a budget. If you get your budgeting right, then you should have a fair idea of what your income and expenditure is likely to be during the year. Let us look briefly at the importance of setting targets and monitoring performance.

Financial control

Good financial results will not arise by happy accident. They will arrive by realistic planning and tight control over expenses.

The figure below illustrates the need for tight controls. Remember that profit is the comparatively small difference between two large numbers: sales and costs. A relatively small change in either costs or sales will, therefore, have a disproportionate effect on profit.

EXAMPLE	Katie's Kitchens: Target v Performance			
		Budget	Change	Actual
	Sales	750,000	–10%	675,000
	less: Direct Costs	375,000	+8%	364,500
	Gross profit	375,000	–17%	310,500
	Overheads	280,000	+10%	308,000
	Net profit	95,000	–97%	2,500

Look what happens if there are a number of relatively small changes. This business was budgeting for a high level of net profit, but a decrease in sales, an unexpected increase in raw material costs of 8 per cent (even allowing for a reduction in raw material usage due to reduced sales) and an increase in overheads of 10 per cent reduces the profit to just £2,500, that is, a reduction of 97 per cent!

You need, therefore, to watch very carefully your costs, prices and margins at all times since small changes in any of these areas can lead to substantial changes in net profit. Control can then be exercised by comparing actual performance with budget. To do this you will need to produce:

11

- A financial plan – agreed as being achievable by all involved. Often the plan will be based on actual performance from the previous year though, as you will see later, it needs to consider other factors also.
- Some means of monitoring performance against the plan. Monitoring will compare monthly accounting 'actuals' with plan projections. It is essential to have an accounting system capable of providing relevant, up-to-date information.

Since there will always be differences between the actual and plan, you need some form of control. Beyond a certain organisational size, control can only be exercised by delegation. The human aspect of control is also important therefore.

Why keep records?

It should already be obvious that accurate record keeping will be required if you are to be effective in monitoring performance against budget. But there are several other reasons why you should keep accurate records. If you are a company there is a statutory obligation to keep financial records and to file annual accounts at Companies House. If the business has shareholders, they will also want accounts so that they can see how well the business is doing. If you are registered for VAT, the VAT inspectors will visit periodically and will want to be convinced that you are accounting for VAT correctly. The Inland Revenue will also want to be assured about your record keeping for the business overall to compute its tax liability and, if you employ people, to ensure that their personal tax and national insurance is being correctly deducted and forwarded to the Collector of Taxes.

If you seek trade terms from suppliers you may find that they require to see previous accounts as part of their assessment of your credit worthiness. In summary, record keeping has to serve four purposes:

- to provide appropriate information for day-to-day management control of the business;
- to provide information which can be used to help in the preparation of next year's plan;
- to provide all the information for the preparation of annual accounts and statutory returns (i.e. Registrar of Companies, Inland Revenue, VAT); and,
- to demonstrate creditworthiness.

The first of these is the most important for monitoring and control of the business. Unfortunately, too many owners and managers believe that they can wait until the end of the year, after which the accountant will tell them how well they are doing. This is a mistake because:

- as already mentioned, published accounts are intended for public consumption (e.g. Inland Revenue, government, shareholders, etc.) and often hide as much as they reveal;
- the annual accounts are historical, often not available until some months after the year to which they relate so any action required will be too late; and,
- the annual accounts do not provide the relevant information for management decisions since these need to be taken on a monthly, weekly or even daily basis.

The accounting records need to be detailed enough to enable you to be able to say at any time what the position of the business is: e.g. How much cash have you in the business? How much do you owe? How much are you owed? How big is your overdraft? How long could you keep on paying the bills if cash stopped flowing into the business? What is your profit margin ?

Conclusion and checklist

For too many businesses, record keeping is driven by external requirements such as the Inland Revenue, the VAT inspectors, or the fact that company law insists that you keep records and file annual accounts. It may help you to think about what financial information is required to help you to control your business and ensure that it is easily available when needed. This book is intended to help you with that thinking. By now you probably recognise the major reasons for keeping tight financial control. These include:

- monitoring performance against plan;
- assessing solvency; and,
- watching liquidity.

If you are able to do all of these effectively and efficiently then you will have the basis of sound financial control. You should be able to avoid unforeseen cash flow problems – instead you will be in a position to visit your bank manager, explain your circumstances and negotiate further loan facilities.

Control will be poor if there is:

- a lack of clear objectives for the business;
- a lack of knowledge of the basic information necessary to run a business successfully;
- a lack of appreciation of the cash needs of the business for a given rate of activity; and
- a tendency to assume that poor results stem from economic conditions or even bad luck.

Are you aware of your current position? Can you, right now, answer all of the following questions.

- What is your net profit on sales?
- What is the return on your capital?
- How much money have you tied up in working capital?
- What is your current bank balance?
- How long do your customers take before they pay?
- Are you solvent?

If you can answer all of those questions then you probably don't need this book. Otherwise, read on.

2

Business objectives

In order to exercise effective control it is important to

- **Agree business objectives and targets.**
- **Set appropriate financial targets and performance measures.**
- **Formulate a budget.**
- **Ensure that managers are accountable.**

Strategic objectives

It is essential for any business to set both long-term and short-term objectives. If you do not have a clear vision of where you are going, you will not know when you get there, nor will you be able to monitor your progress. You also need a clear idea of why you are in business. What is your purpose? Lastly, you need to have some idea of what you are actually going to do to achieve your vision, that is, strategic objectives and how you intend to implement them. Successful businesses are ones that use planning to provide themselves with a framework rather than a straightjacket. They still need to ensure that they can be responsible and flexible when opportunities arise.

> Without an element of planning it is not possible to monitor progress nor, more importantly, to take corrective action when you diverge too far from the plan.[1]

Edward Deming, one of the originators of total quality management, conceived the idea of continuous improvement embodied in the cycle of Plan, Do, Check, Act (PDCA).

---

[1] This chapter gives a brief introduction to strategic thinking and the planning process. If you want to read more see *Planning to Succeed in Business*, David Irwin, Pitman Publishing, 1995.

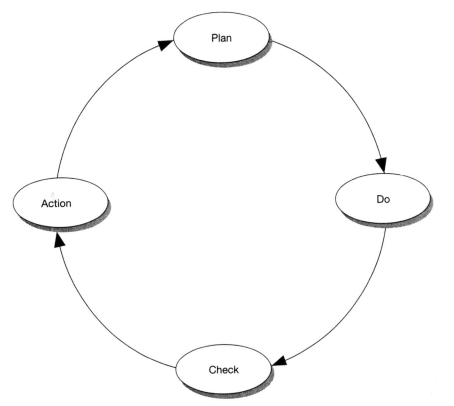

Figure 2.1   PDCA cycle

15

Firstly, set out a plan for what you want to do. Then do it. Check carefully what you have done. Is there scope or need for improvement? If there is, take action dependent on the monitoring. Next time, amend your plan accordingly. It is worth keeping this at the back of your mind in all your planning activities. Planning needs to be a continuous activity if it is to be effective.

Many small businesses think of strategic or long-term planning as something that is only undertaken by large businesses. As stated earlier, the businesses that survive and prosper are those that meet their customers' needs by providing benefits to them at prices which cover the cost to the business of providing the features and also provide both sufficient profit for reinvestment and also a share of the profit or a dividend which satisfies the owners or the shareholders. To do this effectively, Peter Drucker argues[2] that organisations need to focus on the external environment in order to create a customer. Similarly, Michael Porter argues[3] that the way a business positions itself in the market

[2] Peter Drucker, *The Practice of Management*, Heinemann, 1955
[3] Michael Porter, *Competivie Strategy*, Free Press, 1980

place is of paramount importance. More specifically, your task is to match effectively the business's competences (that is, its knowledge, expertise and experience) and resources with the opportunities and threats created by the market place. In other words, businesses should be market driven. Too many businesses or aspiring business people think they can provide a product, but are unsure of whether it is really needed.

Businesses should set a mission and define goals which should ideally define the business's customers as well as what the business does to meet the needs of those customers. The strategy must support the mission, it must fit the environment in which the business works but will be constrained by resource availability. It must also be action focused. In Drucker's words, strategy 'converts what you want to do into accomplishment'. Drucker goes on to argue, therefore, that the two entrepreneurial functions, that is, the two basic functions of any business are marketing and innovation.

For example, 'Blooming Marvellous' describes its purpose as: 'We design, make and market clothes for the fashion-conscious mother-to-be.' With their production skills they could make clothes for anyone, but this statement shows that they have carefully defined their product and their target market.

Large companies inevitably have their mission statements. Many now quote them in their annual reports, though few are as well put as that of Levi Strauss: 'The mission of Levi Strauss is to sustain profitable and responsible commercial success by marketing jeans and selected casual apparel under the Levi brand.'

You may not see a need for a mission statement. It does help, however, to clarify your thinking if you define the purpose of your business and then define targets and time-scales. The purpose (or mission statement) should be the overriding factor in guiding the business. It will help you in defining your marketing and will be of immense value when setting financial objectives. It is not only businesses which set mission statements. Non-profit organisations and charities find them helpful. So do departments or divisions within larger organisations. In setting objectives for the business you may need to satisfy three groups of people, namely: the owners (shareholders), the staff and the customers. Each will have their own expectations.

- The owners will be looking for a return on their capital locked up in the business. This may be yours (and your partners') but you should still be aiming for a better return than you would achieve if the money was, say, in the bank or building society. If you have external investors, they will be looking for capital appreciation and evidence that their investment is being well managed.

- Staff will be looking for realistic rewards for their efforts, career opportunities and an environment in which they are happy to work.
- Customers will be looking for a product or service which represents good value for money. Customers will only pay a premium price for a premium product. You need to take care, therefore, in the positioning of your product in the market place.

Setting overall objectives will be more difficult, therefore, than simply stating that the objective is to operate without making a loss or to maximise profits. Some large companies set themselves targets expressed as ratios, for example, profit per employee, return on equity, profits relative to sales, etc. What is possible will differ between business sectors. Capital intensive businesses, such as property companies, may do well on profit per employee, but badly on return on equity. Service sector businesses, with less equity, show a better return on equity, but make less profit per employee.

You will need to set long-term objectives for your business, such as product introduction, diversification, geographic expansion and market penetration. (Introduce a new product in each of the next three years; have 30 per cent of the local market within six years.) These will then need to be broken down into short-term achievable objectives (such as increase in market share of five per cent per annum). Defining objectives and targets accurately will also assist in monitoring overall performance and in measuring progress. However, remembering that the primary reason for being in business is to make a return on the investment of your time and money, you should set a number of financial and marketing objectives (though marketing objectives are normally translatable into financial ones). These might include, for example:

17

- market share or increase in market share
- growth, measured by level of sales or increase in sales
- level of profit or increase in profit
- profitability, perhaps measured by return on investment or return on equity
- level of productivity or improvement in productivity.

Public limited companies often set targets for earnings per share and for the ratio of share price to earnings (known as the P/E ratio). It is rarely sufficient to set just one of these indicators as an objective.

Setting an objective for turnover alone is never sufficient. You also need an objective for profit. It may well be easier to run a business with a turnover of £100,000 and 20 per cent net profit than one with a turnover of £200,000 and 10 per cent net profit.

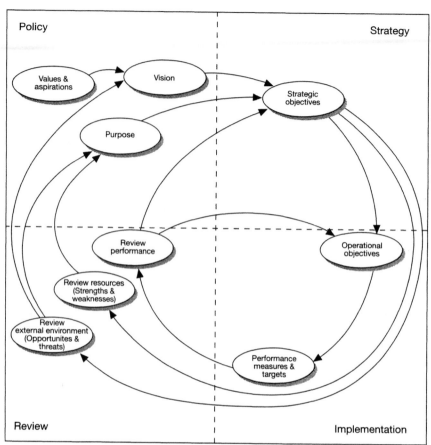

Figure 2.2   Strategic thinking cycle

As you might expect, there are many factors both inside the business (strengths and weaknesses) and outside (opportunities and threats) which will affect ability to achieve your vision and which will therefore influence the strategy you choose to adopt. Michael Porter argues that there are two key elements: the attractiveness of a particular industry defined by the scope for long-term profitability and your competitive position within the industry. Both, of course, change constantly. External influences also affect the strategy and your ability both to fulfil your purpose and to achieve your vision. The market place clearly presents a series of opportunities and threats; opportunities to identify new customer groups and different customer needs but threats from competitors and changes in the way your customers' needs can be addressed.

Who do you see as your customers? Can you define them precisely? How will they perceive your product or service? Have you considered, for example, whether it will be a high quality, high price premium product or a low cost, low price, commodity product? How will you differentiate your business from your competitors? Porter refers to these competitive advantages as *cost leadership* and *differentiation*. Furthermore, you may decide to *focus* your efforts on a fairly narrow segment of the market.

The way you choose to position your product will be reflected in the way that you promote it and in the businesses that you perceive as competitors. It will also affect the way you see external factors and, in particular, opportunities and threats. It may affect the availability of resources. It will certainly affect the way that the business is perceived by its stakeholders including customers, suppliers and the community in which the business operates. All these, in turn, will affect the price that you charge, the quality level you adopt, the cost base you require and the marketing level needed. In short, they will affect your strategic objectives. You may also need to set some non-economic objectives, particularly regarding staff development. Drucker echoes this thinking. He argues that there are eight key areas in which objectives should be set and against which performance should be measured. These are:

19

- market standing
- innovation
- productivity
- physical and financial resources
- profitability
- manager performance and development
- staff performance and attitude
- public responsibility.

Bearing in mind recent legislation on environmental concerns, you may also need an environmental policy and appropriate objectives. Once the strategic objectives have been set, it is possible to define the operational objectives which, in turn, leads to the budget. The budget defines the plan or road-map for the business, but it also gives the information needed for effective control. The Plan Do Check Act cycle introduced earlier can be redrawn to help you to think about the important elements of budgeting and control.

The planning part of the cycle requires you to set objectives for the business and to translate those objectives into financial objectives: a budget. Devising that budget will require consideration of costing and pricing, of capital expenditure requirements and of the likely timing of receipts and payments. This is all covered in part three of this book.

During the next stage, the 'doing' stage, you will be doing whatever it is that your business does. But you will also be recording financial information: income and expenditure; receipts and payments; assets and liabilities. This requires an effective book-keeping system. An introduction to book-keeping is given in Chapter 8.

The third stage is to review actual performance by comparing it with the plan. Some suggestions for this checking are offered in Chapter 9. If there are major differences then you will need to take corrective action. If you undertake those three stages effectively, then you will be in control of your business.

Part two of the book is intended to assist those readers who would like a refresher on understanding the figures found in financial statements and which will be used constantly in the rest of the book.

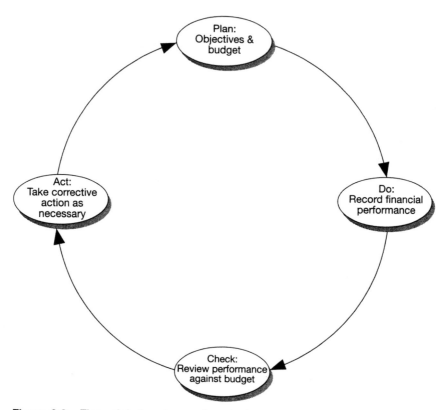

Figure 2.3   Financial planning and control

Operational objectives

Strategic objectives have the danger of being too far removed from everyday reality for people to keep them in mind as they work. They also tend to be set for the medium to long term rather than for the short term. It is essential therefore to break them down into clear and explicit operational objectives with timescales, performance measures and targets. The operational objectives may simply be milestones along a route towards achieving a strategic objective – for example, raising sales by 20 per cent per annum on the way to doubling sales turnover. They should always provide quantitative and/or qualitative targets so that performance can be measured. In effect, the operational objectives should provide the following year's business plan.

As with the vision, operational objectives should be challenging, achievable and measurable. Don't have too many operational objectives, otherwise they become difficult to monitor. And remember to think about the assumptions on which your strategy is based. It is very easy for managers in businesses to adopt systems or mechanisms which they think will improve their ability to manage.

> Remember that a key element of effective management is managing and motivating people and that any system can only provide some support.

21

Ideally, however, you will want an integrated management system which enables the setting of strategic objectives, planning and forecasting, recording data, comparing performance against plan and exercising control. Financial control needs to be part of that management system, but it also needs to be something for which all staff have a responsibility.

Unless you are working on your own, therefore, you need to build your staff into a team who are all pulling in the same direction for the good of the business. Each person must have a job that is directed towards fulfilling the objectives of the whole business. The aim, in management by objectives, is to agree mutually a set of objectives for every person in the business. These need to be precise ('increase your sales by 5 per cent by volume', rather than 'increase sales'), challenging and achievable. If the targets are unrealistic then people will not even try; on the other hand, people need to be stretched. These objectives then become the yardstick by which individual performance can be measured.

Remember that the human aspect is very important. The following pointers may help in reaching agreement for the business objectives.

- Individual responsibility and individual accountability is essential. Each department or activity must be the sole responsibility of just one person. This avoids buck-passing or confusion as to who is responsible. Moreover, that person must have the authority to exercise control. Responsibility and authority go hand in hand.

- If individuals are to work to a plan, they must feel committed to that plan. They will only be committed if they were consulted in the initial stages. If they had the opportunity to influence the original plan, then they will have a high degree of commitment to the outcome. As stated earlier, all targets must be achievable.

- Normally, each person is responsible for controlling some small part of the total. It can be a great help if every individual is aware of how their part interacts with the remainder, and why failure in one area (theirs) will affect others.

- Each person can only do so much. Their efforts should be focused where they will yield the greatest result. There is a very real danger of trying to exercise too much control over too many things. The principle of management by exception (i.e. looking for variances from expectations and aiming to make corrections) is a sound one.

- Ensure individuals are made aware of the results of their efforts. Praise regularly.

22

EXERCISE

Setting strategic objectives

Sit quietly and think about where you want your business to be in, say, five years' time. How are you going to get there? Once you start to answer those questions, you are well on the way to setting strategic and operational objectives.

Budgeting

Once the financial objectives have been set, it is possible to prepare and agree a budget. A budget should restate the overall plan in figures. It is different to a forecast in the sense that the plan, and therefore the budget, sets minimum requirements, whereas a forecast is usually an expectation of what is most likely to happen. You might choose to budget for sales of £180,000 and you use this figure in calculating your likely expenditure, profit, etc. Based on your market research however you forecast sales of £200,000. You set a sales target of £220,000 in order to stretch your sales force. If all your costs are covered by the budgeted figure, then you will make a greater profit if you achieve the forecast and greater still if you achieve the target. While this is an important distinction, in practice for most businesses the forecast and budget will be the same.

Budgets are generally only set for the short term – say, to the end of the next financial year. The starting point is the sales forecast – how many products at what price, where and when. This can then be turned into a sales budget. The budget commits the business to at least perform to that standard. It should, therefore, be achievable but challenging, just as with the objectives for measuring individual members of staff. Once the sales budget has been prepared it is possible to produce a production budget (direct costs) and a resources budget (overhead costs). These can be combined to give a cash budget, a capital budget and a budgeted profit and loss account. We will return to budgeting in Chapter 7.

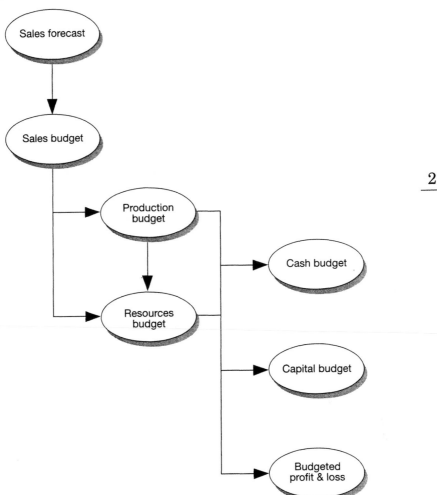

23

Figure 2.4   Budgeting

The budget will only be as good as the work you put into it, but it is there to help you manage and control the business. You must use it to review performance regularly. If the business is going off course, shown by variances from the budget, then you will need to take corrective action. All corrective action needs to be flexible, however. Major changes in one area may alter the performance in another. It is important that management and staff all participate in the budget setting exercise; this will help in ensuring that everyone 'owns' the targets and that everyone understands why expenses have to be controlled.

Accounting centres

The importance of individual accountability was mentioned earlier. This requires you to delegate authority and responsibility. One way of giving financial responsibility to individuals is to set up a system of accounting centres. (You may have heard the terms profit centre, cost centre and investment centre – inevitably some functions do not make a profit and tend to be scorned by those that do – so I prefer a neutral term.)

Where businesses make a range of more than one product, each product is often split into a separate accounting centre. Not only does this devolve some of the financial responsibility, it also makes it easier to determine which products are profitable. Some costs, such as factory rent, are more difficult to allocate so these are often recorded in a holding account and then split on some arbitrary but fair basis between the different products. The indirect costs may be allocated, for example, by the proportion of total sales represented by each product (by volume or cost), or by proportion of machine time used, or by some other appropriate method.

While this split will give at least an indication of the profitability of each product, beware of the temptation to cease sales of a particular product because profit is too low or there is an apparent loss. In most cases, the effect of eliminating one product will be to spread the indirect costs over fewer products; thus, sales of the other products may need to be increased as a result. It is essential, however, to ensure that all products are making a contribution.

There are four possible levels of financial responsibility with appropriate targets and control requirements.

Revenue centre

In a revenue centre, staff only have responsibility for income. A typical revenue centre might be a sales department in a department store. Staff have set sales targets and it is income that is measured and compared with the targets.

24

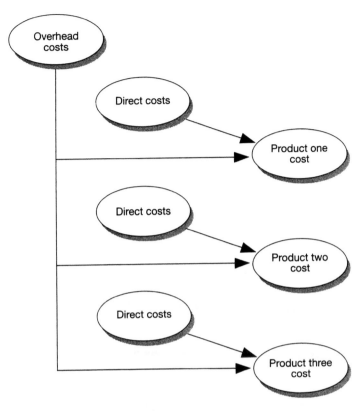

Figure 2.5   Allocating overheads

Cost centre

In a cost centre, on the other hand, staff only have responsibility for keeping costs within the set targets. They do not have to worry about from where the money comes. An NHS Trust department, for example, might be a cost centre.

Profit centre

In a profit centre, staff have rather more responsibility but rather more control also. A profit centre might be, for example, a division within a larger company. They will agree targets of profitability and absolute level of profit. Control will usually be through monitoring performance as measured by the profit and loss account. They are unable, however, to invest in new equipment.

Investment centre

An investment centre has more control still. An investment centre might typically be a subsidiary company. In an investment centre the staff have authority over investments and the use of assets, though major investments may be subject to approval by the holding company. Targets would focus on return on capital and control would be through monitoring performance measured by the complete accounts.

As suggested earlier, it will assist in the planning process if the individual responsible for each accounting centre (if you decide to use them) is involved in preparing plans and budgets. Whether to use accounting centres needs, therefore, to be determined at an early stage.

Conclusion and checklist

It is important for every business to think carefully about where it wants to go and to have a clear plan. The plan needs to be flexible enough to enable the business to respond to opportunities as they appear, but it also needs to set a framework to help all the staff to know what is expected of them. Typically, the plan will define for the business:

- Its key purpose and its vision for the future.
- The strategic objectives to achieve the vision.
- Operational objectives to lead towards the achievement of the strategic objectives.
- Financial objectives.
- A budget (for the business and for individual managers).

There are four essential aspects of budgeting and control:

- Involve all responsible personnel.
- Produce a viable business plan and appropriate financial forecast.
- Have an accounting system capable of monitoring performance against the plan.
- Have a system of management controls capable of keeping the business on the right track.

26

Part 2

■

Understanding the figures

Financial statements

> Effective control requires effective planning and target setting but it also requires an understanding of financial statements and an ability to interpret the figures. This chapter explains
>
> - Profit and loss accounts.
> - Balance sheets.
> - Cash flow statements.
> - The relationship between the financial statements.

If you are already familiar with financial statements you may prefer to skip this chapter. On the other hand you may feel that you would benefit from a brief refresher. If so, read on.

Financial statements

There are three basic financial statements which describe the activities and financial state of any business:

- The *profit and loss account* (P&L) shows how a business performed over a specific period and reveals the total revenue and total expenditure related to that period.
- The *balance sheet* summarises the state of a business at a specific date. Balance sheets are linked by a P&L which covers the period between the two dates.
- The *cash flow statement* summarises cash receipts to and cash payments from the business. A forecast of cash flow is one of the most important management accounting tools. It provides an estimate of the business's cash requirements for the next trading period.

Accounting simply follows the money flowing within, to and from a business. It is important to remember that the accounts reflect the finances of the business, not of the owner(s). It is often helpful to split up funds within a business to show sources and applications. Sources show from where the money has come; applications show to where the

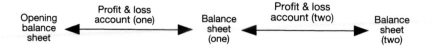

Figure 3.1   Financial statements

money has gone. Until a few years ago, British balance sheets showed *finance* or *liabilities*, that is, sources on the left and *assets*, that is applications, on the right. (The rest of Europe and the US reverse the columns to show sources on the right and applications on the left.) As you will see later, balance sheets now tend to be set out in a single column. It can, however, still be helpful to think about sources and applications in separate columns.

Source of funds	Application of funds

In double entry book-keeping every financial transaction requires two entries normally with each entry in a different ledger with the entries balancing one another. In other words, as will be illustrated shortly, the sources and applications need to balance.

Profit and loss account

A profit and loss account (P&L) shows what happened in a business, in terms of sales, other income and expenditure, during a specific period. All businesses have to prepare a profit and loss account at least once each year, as part of their annual accounts. In that case the P&L covers a year's activities. However they can be prepared for any period of time. The P&L shows:

- The revenue (that is, the income of the business) for the period.
- The expenditure for the period.
- How much profit there was (after deducting all the allowable expenses from the revenue).
- How the profit has been divided.

The largest and often the only source of funds to a business, on a regular basis, is the revenue produced by sales. A large proportion of the revenue is applied to cover the business's expenditure.

Source of funds	Application of funds
Revenues	Expenses

The sales figure reflects the revenue from actual sales of products or services during the period, excluding VAT; it does not reflect the cash received from customers since some payments may still be outstanding or have been deposited in advance. (N.B. for businesses registered for VAT, the output tax (i.e. VAT on sales) is exactly equal to the input tax (i.e. tax on purchases) plus the tax handed over to the government. In other words, VAT in and VAT out exactly balance with no benefit or deficit to the business.)

Businesses may not receive cash for their sales until 30 or 60 days or even longer after the sale is made. The sale is recorded immediately on the profit and loss account, although the cash is not available for use by the business until it is received. Expenditure on overheads is usually recorded immediately on the P&L, but it must be recorded for the period to which it relates. Business may not actually pay for goods or services until well after they have been provided. This is known as *accrued* expenditure. Some payments, however, may represent pre-payment. For example, rent or insurance, paid in advance, may partly relate to the current period and partly to the following period.

Direct costs, sometimes known as *cost of sales*, are the costs that can be directly attributed to the production of a particular product or services. The direct costs will clearly vary depending on the level of production. In other words the direct costs should reflect raw materials, direct labour and sub-contract costs in the product or service actually sold during the period. There may be stock purchased during the period which was not consumed; this will be shown on the balance sheet but not charged to the profit and loss account. Similarly, stock may have been consumed during the period but purchased in an earlier period.

Suppose you purchase raw materials worth £1,000. You now have stock worth £1,000 but you have not yet incurred expenditure which can be shown on the P&L. You then turn those raw materials into a finished product. As long as the products remain unsold, you will still have a stock value for them and do not show expenditure on the P&L. As soon as you sell a product, however, you immediately record both the income for the product and the raw material's cost. Subtracting the direct costs from the revenue gives the *gross profit*, also known as the *contribution*, because it contributes towards paying for the overheads (and once the overheads are all paid, it contributes to profit).

31

Source of funds		Application of funds	
Revenues		Expenses	
Sales	10,000	Raw Materials & Overheads	8,000
		Retained earnings	2,000
	10,000		10,000

The example shows revenue from sales of £10,000. Raw materials and overheads require expenditure of £8,000 which leaves a net profit of £2,000 which for the moment has been retained in the business. Now look at the example of Young & Co's Brewery plc. Sales of £72m in 1993/4 produced a gross profit, or a contribution, of nearly £50m.

Young & Co's Brewery plc
Profit & Loss Account for the year ended 2 April 1994

	£'000	£'000
Sales		72,300
Raw materials	15,000	
Excise duty	7,700	
		22,700
Gross profit		49,600
Employment costs	21,900	
Depreciation	4,000	
Other operating costs	15,800	
		41,700
Profit before interest and tax		7,900
Interest payable		2,700
Profit before tax		5,200
Tax		1,700
Profit after tax		3,500
Dividends		2,000
Retained earnings		1,500

32

The *gross profit margin* is simply the gross profit divided by sales and usually expressed as a percentage. The overheads are deducted from the gross profit to give the *net profit*, sometimes referred to as profit before interest and tax (PBIT) and sometimes as trading profit. In turn, the *net profit margin* is the net profit divided by sales and expressed as a percentage. For Young & Co, the gross profit margin is 68 per cent and the net profit margin is 11 per cent.

If you have set up a company, or if you are a manager in any business, then your salary, together with the salaries of all your staff, will be treated as expenses. However, if you are self-employed (as a sole trader or a partner) the money available to you is the *profit*, i.e. the revenue less all the costs. You will need to draw money out from the business on a regular basis. Remember that your *drawings* are simply an advance against profit. You are taxed on all the profit (after deducting any interest due). For the purpose of calculating costs, however, it makes sense to treat your drawings and any income tax as overhead costs.[1]

Note that some businesses show the deduction of interest, particularly for long-term loans, after calculating profit. This can be particularly helpful since it makes it easier to calculate return on capital and draw conclusions about the business's performance. If you decide to show interest after the net profit do not forget to include it as an overhead in your costing and pricing calculations.

Depreciation is always charged to the profit and loss account to show that the use of fixed assets is one of the costs of generating income. It is an allocation of the cost of the fixed assets over their useful, or income generating, lives. Depreciation does not involve the receipt or payment of cash; it is a book entry. It is important, however, that money is put on one side. Otherwise you may not have the resources available when you do need to replace the equipment.

33

> Capital introduced by the owners, loans and loan repayments are not shown on the profit and loss account since they do not represent income or expenditure.

Matching revenues and costs

The concept of accruals has been touched on already. It often confuses though, in fact, is quite simple. Let us look first at sales. Sales income is not the same as cash received. A sale is normally recorded at the time that the goods are dispatched or a service provided, irrespective of whether the customer has paid. In VAT terms, this is the tax point. If a sale has been effected, but no cash has yet been received, the monies owing will be shown on the balance sheet as a debtor. All the sales during the period are summarised as income in the profit and loss account.

For long-term contracts, especially in the construction industry, some businesses treat work in progress as work done and show it as income on their profit or loss account. In this case, care needs to be

---

[1] You may hear people refer to fixed costs, variable costs and indirect costs. To avoid confusion, this book will refer to overheads to describe all those costs which are not direct costs.

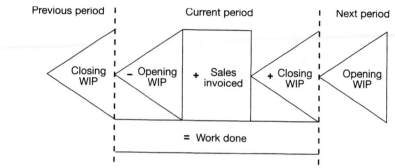

Figure 3.2   Accruals principle (sales)

taken only to count the income once. The total work done is, therefore, equal to invoiced sales less the opening work in progress brought from the previous period plus the closing work in progress carried forward to the next period. It is only the raw materials that goes into the work done that are recorded as materials consumed, that is, cost of sales. The closing stock from one period will be the opening stock for the next period. The materials consumed equals the materials purchased plus the opening stocks brought down from the previous period less the closing stocks carried forward to the next period. The cost of sales is shown on the profit and loss account but the stock is shown on the balance sheet until it is consumed.

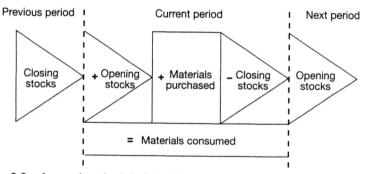

Figure 3.3   Accruals principle (stock)

Similarly overheads are charged to the profit and loss account according to when the resources are used, not when cash is paid. For example, rent of £12,000 for a two-year period could be paid in advance; the profit and loss account for the first year will include rent of £6,000 as only that amount is attributable to the first period. The balance will be a prepayment. There may also be some accrued expenses. The overhead costs incurred are the overheads paid for plus the opening prepayments brought down less the closing prepayments carried forward less the opening accruals brought down plus the closing accruals carried forward. The balance sheet shows prepayments and accruals as current assets and current liabilities respectively.

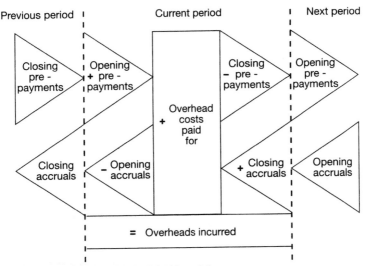

Figure 3.4   Accruals principle (overheads)

These three elements can be summarised as shown in Figure 3.5. The work done less the materials consumed less the overheads incurred equals the profit.

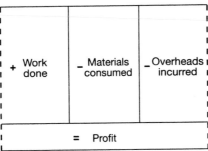

Figure 3.5   Accruals principle (summary)

Appropriation account

It is normal at the bottom of a P&L account to show an *appropriation account*, that is, an explanation of how the profit is divided. Profit can be divided in just three ways: to the shareholders or owners (as dividends or drawings); to the government as tax; or, it might be retained in the business (to use as working capital or to buy equipment or other assets). Remembering that interest is usually also deducted from profit we can summarise as follows:

- Profit before interest and tax (PBIT)
- Deduct interest to give: Profit before tax (PBT)
- Deduct tax to give: Profit after tax (PAT)
- Deduct dividend to give: Retained earnings (RE) which are transferred to reserves on the balance sheet.

EXERCISE

Katie's Kitchens: Profit and loss

Katie owns a company which manufactures and markets kitchen units. She sells to kitchen installers but does not do installation herself nor does she supply any of the electrical, gas or other fittings. For the year to 31 December 1994, Katie achieved considerable success with the running of her business. Her sales topped the million for the first time reaching £1.1m.

Her direct costs were 50 per cent of sales. Wages including Katie's own salary were fixed at £20,000 per month. Her other overheads including premises, marketing and distribution costs totalled £119,000 for the year. She also had depreciation of £11,000 in 1994. The business paid loan and overdraft interest of £25,000. She expects to pay corporation tax on her profit after interest at a rate of 25 per cent and has decided to pay a dividend this year, for the first time, to the shareholders. The dividend will total £15,000.

Prepare a profit and loss account showing the business's performance for 1994.
- What is the net profit margin?
- How much of the profit is retained in the business?

The solution to this exercise is shown on page 188. Katie's Kitchens will be used for more exercises later in the book so you might like to keep your solution handy for ease of reference.

Balance Sheet

What a business owns (its assets) is always equal to what it owes (its liabilities). It is the liabilities that are used to finance the business. The starting point for every business is zero.

36

Source of funds	Application of funds
Liabilities	Assets

Imagine that you put £10,000 into a business. That £10,000 is effectively owed to you, but it is also used to finance the assets of the business. Initially it might be held as *cash in bank*, that is, an asset. If the business then spends £7,000 on equipment, it has fixed assets of £7,000 and cash in bank of £3,000, still totalling £10,000.

Source of funds		Application of funds	
Liabilities		Assets	
Owners	10,000	Cash in bank	3,000
		Equipment	7,000
Total finance	10,000	Total assets	10,000

37

A balance sheet is a financial 'snapshot' which summarises the assets and liabilities of a business at a specific point in time.

It is simply the summary of the balances from each of the ledgers referred to earlier[2]. All businesses have to prepare a balance sheet at least once each year, as part of their annual accounts, but a balance sheet can be prepared at any time. It incorporates how much the business owes to suppliers and how much is due from customers. It reflects assets such as equipment and vehicles used in the business, the level of stock and the amount of capital you have invested in the business.

The balance sheet shows:

- How much capital is employed in the business (How much is the business worth and from where has the capital come?)
- How quickly assets can be turned into cash (How liquid is the business?)
- How solvent the business is. (What is the likelihood that the business might become insolvent?)
- How the business is financed. (Where does the finance come from and how much of it is debt?)

Let us look at an example, once again using figures from Young & Co's Brewery, in the sources and applications format used so far.

[2] A slightly more detailed explanation is provided in Chapter 8 in the section on double entry book-keeping.

Young & Co's Brewery plc
Balance Sheet as at 2 April 1994

	£'000			£'000
Capital & Reserves			Fixed assets	153,100
Share capital	7,800			
Share premium account	1,500			
Revaluation reserve	87,100			
Retained earnings	20,400			
		116,800		
Loans				
Long-term loans	29,000			
Deferred taxation	3,300			
		32,300		
Current liabilities			Current assets	
Short-term loans	3,400		Stock	4,000
Trade creditors	2,800		Debtors	5,500
Other creditors	7,500		Cash	200
		13,700		9,700
Total finance		162,800	Total assets	162,800

In this business the owners (i.e. the shareholders) have bought shares which at par were worth nearly £8m. Some investors, however, paid a premium to the company totalling £1.5m. Buildings owned by the company have been revalued since their acquisition. This has resulted in the creation of a reserve fund of £87m which represents the difference between acquisition price and the value at the date of the revaluation. Lastly, it has retained earnings of over £20m. There are long-term borrowings of £29m (and deferred taxation of £3m which is effectively on loan from the government) and short-term liabilities of nearly £14m.

All of this has been used to finance fixed assets with a valuation of £153m and current assets of nearly £10m. Now let us look at each of the terms in turn:

Fixed assets are generally assets with a life longer than one year. For most businesses, all the fixed assets will be tangible assets such as equipment and buildings. The cost of tangible fixed assets is depreciated over the expected lives of the assets; it is quite common to see the original cost of tangible assets together with their accumulated depreciation shown on a balance sheet. Fixed assets may also include intangible assets such as *goodwill* or expenditure on research which has been capitalised. It is now regarded as good practice to write these off as quickly as possible; ideally, they should be written off as expenditure immediately. It is, however, not always possible to write off goodwill in one go without making the balance sheet look sick although lenders will always ignore goodwill. Research and development costs for contracts which are firm and which will last more than one year may be capitalised and depreciated over the term of the contract.

Gordon's News

You buy a newsagency with a net worth of £30,000 and an annual profit of £50,000. You agree to pay £75,000. This represents purchase of the assets of £30,000 and goodwill of £45,000.

Current assets and *current liabilities* usually have a life of less than one year. Current assets include stock, work in progress, debtors, cash at bank, etc. *Debtors* (known in the US as receivables) represent the amount of money owed to the business by its customers. Current liabilities include creditors, overdrafts, loans due within one year, money owed under hire purchase agreements, any amounts owed in VAT or tax, etc. Creditors, sometimes called trade creditors (and payables in the US) represent the amount of money owed by the business to suppliers. The creditors' figure is largely, usually, the money specifically owing for raw materials and sub-contract costs. Loans falling due in more than one year are usually shown separately. You may prefer, however, to show all loans as current liabilities. For small businesses this will generally give a better idea of the business's performance. Accountants always used to prepare balance sheets in the two-column style shown above. It is more normal, these days, to show the balance sheet as a single column. There are advantages with both.

Look again at the example above. Move current liabilities to the right and subtract it from current assets to give net current assets. Add the fixed assets. Then move long-term loans to the right and subtract it from the previous figure. This gives net assets. Net assets is equal to the owners' finance which is also moved to the right but shown at the bottom. Now look at the example on page 40:

The *total assets* of the business are the fixed assets plus the current assets. In the first illustration, note that it is the total of the right-hand side of the figure. (Note that total assets also equals the left-hand side, that is owners' funds plus long-term loans plus current liabilities). *Net current assets*, also known by accountants as working capital, is simply the difference between current assets and current liabilities. This should be positive, otherwise the business may not be able to meet debts as they fall due. In the example, it is negative and is known as net current liabilities. The term, working capital, can be slightly confusing since the amount of working capital needed by the business will vary. Remember that the balance sheet is only a snapshot – and the business may need a higher level of working capital than ever shown on the balance sheet.

Young & Co's Brewery plc
Balance Sheet as at 2 April 1994

	£'000	£'000
Fixed assets		153,100
Current assets		
Stock	4,000	
Debtors	5,500	
Cash	200	
	9,700	
Current liabilities		
Short-term loans	3,400	
Trade creditors	2,800	
Other creditors	7,500	
	13,700	
Net current assets (liabilities)		(4,000)
Total assets less current liabilities		149,100
less: long-term loans and deferred taxation		32,300
Net assets		116,800
Capital & reserves	7,800	
Share premium account	1,500	
Revaluation reserve	87,100	
Retained earnings	20,400	
Net finance		116,800

The example shows the creditors falling due after more than one year deducted to show the net assets of the business. This will probably only include bank loans and HP payments due in more than 12 months. Deducting this figure from the net current liabilities gives the *net assets* of the business. The net assets should be equal to the total capital and reserves, that is, the *net worth*, sometimes known as *net finance* or the *equity* of the business. This comprises the money introduced by the shareholders or owners and the retained earnings. Normally, for a small business, the reserves are simply the retained profits. The term is often misunderstood: reserves show where the money came from, not how it has been used. It may exist as cash in the bank, but more likely it will have been used to buy more equipment or to add to working capital, that is, to finance stock and work in progress. On balance sheets in this book, I will use the term retained earnings in an effort to avoid any misunderstanding.

The net worth, together with any long-term loans, is called the *capi-*

tal employed. The distinction between total finance (which equals total assets) and capital employed is that the capital employed excludes all short-term liabilities. Look again at the two-column balance sheet on page 38. Note that moving current liabilities to the right-hand side leaves capital employed on the left equal to net assets on the right. Current liabilities include short-term loans and overdrafts. Since for smaller businesses short-term borrowing tends to be a large proportion of total borrowing, I suggest that all borrowing is included when calculating capital employed.

Sources of funds	Application of funds
Capital employed — Net worth — • Retained earnings • Owner's finance • (Long term) loans	Total assets — • Fixed assets
• Current liabilities	• Current liabilities

Figure 3.6   Balance sheet summary

The figure summarises from where the money comes, which can only be three sources:

- retained earnings, that is, profit which has been generated by and retained within the business
- equity introduced by the owner(s)
- loans (whether from the bank or effectively, from creditors).

EXERCISE

Katie's Kitchens – Balance Sheet

Let us return to Katie's Kitchens and prepare balance sheets to show both her opening position at the beginning of 1994 and her closing position at the end of that year. By the end of December 1993, Katie had equipment with a net book value of £56,000. (It cost originally £80,000 and had accumulated depreciation of £24,000.) She originally invested £45,000 of her own (and her family's) money in the business.

At 31 December 1993 Katie had stock (mostly wood) which cost £25,000 (ex VAT). She had trade debtors of £150,000 and £35,000 in the bank but owed Customs & Excise £25,000 in value added tax and had trade creditors of £50,000. Katie's Kitchens had a modest year in 1993 making a profit of £95,000 before interest and tax. Interest both on the term loan and on the occasional overdraft cost £24,000 and there was tax due of £17,750; Katie decided not to pay a dividend for the year. As a result, the profit retained in the business was £53,250. In addition, she had a term loan from the bank of

£75,000 which is being repaid at the rate of £2,500 per month. Prepare a balance sheet showing the position of Katie's Kitchens on 31 December 1993.

- What is the net worth of the business?
- What is the level of capital employed?
- What is the level of total assets?

Now have a further look at the information provided in the last exercise and at the profit and loss account you derived. Prepare a balance sheet for 31 December 1994. In addition you will need to know that the level of stock has increased to £45,000, debtors have increased to £180,000 and creditors have increased to £64,750. The outstanding VAT amount has fallen to £20,000. Katie spent £40,000 on additional premises and capital equipment during the year. The tax for 1993 was paid during 1994, but the tax for 1994 and the dividend will be paid during 1995.

- What is the new level of cash in the business ?
- What is the level of capital employed ?

Cash flow statements

Reference has already been made to cash flow. A cash flow statement simply shows out all the receipts to and payments by the business. Cash flow statements for historical periods usually show what happened for a year though, as with other statements, they can be prepared for any period. The cash flow statement shows how money flowed into and out of the business during the year and relates the profit and loss statement to the balance sheet. In particular, it shows by how much the working capital in the business increased or decreased and highlights the reasons for the changes. It does not show the amount of working capital available; that is on the balance sheet. Remember that a cash flow statement only shows cash in and cash out, so non-cash items such as depreciation are ignored.

Source of funds	*Application of funds*
Receipts	Payments

It sometimes seems strange to people who are not accountants that a business can be profitable and yet be short of money or running an overdraft. It must be remembered that profit and cash are not the same.

You will recall that the profit and loss account matches revenues and expenses for a specific period though the revenues accrued for that period may not all have been received nor the expenses all paid. If, for example a business receives cash of £5,000 in respect of sales and has to pay out £6,000 in expenses, then it will have to borrow £1,000 from the bank (or from the owners), even though the level of sales may, in reality, be far higher.

Source of funds		Application of funds	
Receipts		Payments	
Debtors	5,000	Wages	3,000
Bank loan	1,000	Cash purchases	3,000
	6,000		10,000

A typical example taken from Young & Co's Brewery is shown below. Before looking at the example, return to the profit and loss account and the balance sheets for Young & Co and see if you can make a stab at producing the cash flow statement.

43

CASE STUDY

Young & Co's Brewery plc
Statement of cash flow

	Notes	£'000	£'000
Net cash inflow from operating activities	a		12,300
Returns on investments and servicing of finance			
Interest received		0	
Interest paid		(3,000)	
Dividends paid		(2,000)	
			(5,000)
Taxation			
Corporation tax paid		(1,400)	
Tax paid			(1,400)
Investing activities			
Payments to acquire intangible fixed assets			
Payments to acquire tangible fixed assets		(4,800)	
Receipts from sales of tangible fixed assets		300	
Other		(100)	
			(4,600)
Net cash inflow before financing			1,300
Financing			
Issue of ordinary share capital			
Receipts from new borrowings	b	(15,000)	
Debenture issue costs	b	300	
Repayments of borrowings	b	14,600	
Net cash inflow from financing			(100)
Increase in cash and cash equivalents	c		1,400
			1,300

It may not be immediately obvious how some of the figures in the cash flow statement have been derived, so the annual accounts will usually also have some notes to explain and reconcile the figures. As can be seen, Young & Co's working capital has increased by £1.3m. Cash has improved by £1.4m and the stock position by £0.9m, but the debtors' position has deteriorated by £0.5m.

Notes to the cash flow statement

(a) Reconciliation of operating profit to net cash inflow from operating activities

	£'000
Operating profit	7,900
Depreciation	4,000
Profit on disposal of fixed assets	
(Increase)/decrease in stocks	900
(Increase)/decrease in debtors	(500)
Increase/(decrease) in creditors	
Net cash inflow from operating activities	12,300

(b) Analysis of changes in financing during the period

	Short term	More than one year	Total
	£'000	£'000	£'000
At beginning of period	7,700	26,300	34,000
Repayments of borrowing	(2,600)	(12,000)	(14,600)
Net proceeds from new borrowings		14,700	14,700
Movement in bank overdraft (see note c)	(1,800)		(1,800)
At the end of the period	3,300	29,000	32,300

(c) Analysis of the balances of cash and cash equivalents as shown on the balance sheet

	1994	Change	1993
	£'000		£'000
Cash at bank and in hand	100	(400)	500
Bank overdrafts	(2,300)	1,800	(4,100)
	(2,200)	1,400	(3,600)

Cash flow statements can be used to keep an eye on competitors. For example, if firms are spending more on capital equipment than their depreciation charge suggests, they may be expanding. If their working capital has increased it may simply be because of inflation, or poor control of stocks or debtors, or it might point to expansion. If working capital decreases, it might be because of a contraction in business, or a trading loss, or it might be because control of stock and debtors has improved. If working capital has decreased, it may to lead to problems of liquidity. Cash flows are particularly helpful to businesses when they are used as forecasts. They can then be used to summarise targets and to monitor performance. We will return to this in Chapter 7.

EXERCISE

Katie's Kitchens – Cashflow statement

You should have sufficient information from the two previous exercises to prepare a cash flow statement for Katie's Kitchens showing receipts and payments for 1994. Remember that figures for debtors and creditors include VAT owed by customers and to suppliers.

45

Conclusion

An integral part of planning and making decisions is a comprehensive understanding of the current position of your business – financial statements are the most effective tools for monitoring your current position. The three types of financial statements – profit and loss account, balance sheet and cash flow statement – enable you to monitor your finances; they also provide information which you can use as the basis of calculating performance indicators such as ratios. These will be covered in the next chapter.

The profit and loss account records the total revenue and total expenditure related to a specific period. It is this statement that monitors the profitability of the business – whether the level of sales are sufficiently high and the level of expenditure is sufficiently low.

The balance sheet, by summarising the different types of assets and liabilities of a business, indicates how much finance is tied up and what level of working capital there is. From this, it is possible to monitor liquidity and solvency.

The cash flow statement is most useful when written as a forecast. By calculating budgets for prospective sales, costs and schedules, it is possible to establish when there will be a cash flow deficit. If this is foreseen, then arrangements can be made to borrow money for working capital – arranging an overdraft, for example. Monitoring performance against the cash flow forecast will also help to identify other problems; corrective action can then be taken as required.

The relationship between these three types of financial statements is illustrated in Figure 3.7. In the next chapter we will be looking at ratio analysis and added value analysis which can be used to interpret accounts in more detail. An understanding of ratios will also help in setting targets for the business's performance.

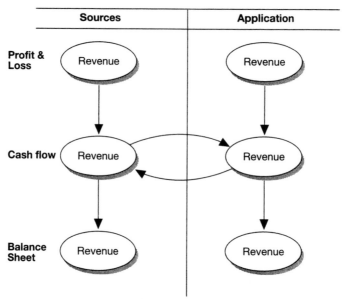

Figure 3.7   Sources and applications summary

4

Interpreting accounts

- **Ratio analysis can be immensely helpful in interpreting the financial position of any business.**
- **Ratios can also be used to set targets and to measure performance.**
- **Added value analysis will give a feel for the wealth being created by the business.**

Chapter 3 explained how to read the main financial statements of a business. However, it is only when you start to analyse the figures that they begin to reveal a true picture of the business.

Ratio analysis

Many people find it difficult to look at a profit and loss account or a balance sheet and derive a full picture. As a result, ratios are often used to interpret accounts. A ratio is simply a relationship between two numbers. They indicate how a business is performing and also provide indications of trends and patterns.

They can be compared to the same ratios in previous years' accounts and the accounts of other businesses operating in a similar environment. Ratios are published for many business sectors which can be used as a comparison (these are sometimes referred to as *Industry Norms*[1]).

This chapter will primarily concentrate on the use of ratios in analysing accounts. It will, however, conclude with some thoughts on using ratios for target setting and performance measurement. We will return to this in Chapter 7 which looks at formulating the financial aspect of the business plan. For convenience, I have split the ratios described in this chapter into five somewhat arbitrary groups:

[1] See for example figures produced by Centre for Interfirm Comparisons or ICC Business Publications

- *Profitability* – how good is the business as an investment.
- *Solvency* – how near is the business to bankruptcy.
- *Liquidity* – the amount of working capital available.
- *Efficiency* – how good is the management of the business.
- Staff performance and productivity ratios.

Profitability

The most important objectives for the business and, arguably there-fore, the most important ratios, are those concerned with profitability. You will want to ensure that your gross profit is sufficient to cover all your overhead costs, and your drawings if you are self-employed, and to generate an additional profit to retain within the business to rein-vest and to provide additional working capital. You will also need to generate sufficient cash to repay any loans that might be outstanding. As well as defining levels of profit in absolute terms it is usual to look at profitability as a ratio of profit to sales.

Gross profit margin is one objective that should be set at the outset of the business and then closely monitored.

$$Gross\ profit\ margin = \frac{gross\ profit}{sales} \times 100\%$$

If your gross profit margin starts to drop you might be paying too much for raw materials or you might be having to discount your sales price too much to achieve sales. Many businesses also set a target for net profit margin. This ratio uses profit before interest and tax (PBIT).

$$Net\ profit\ margin = \frac{PBIT}{sales} \times 100\%$$

If you are self-employed, rather than a director in a company, the net profit is shown before drawings are deducted. In order to compare your business with others it might make sense for you to deduct drawings to give your trading profit and use that figure to calculate the ratio. Obtaining published accounts for your competitors can reveal a great deal about their performance. While it is often difficult to determine their gross profit margin, it is relatively easy to discover their net profit margin. You can use this to benchmark your performance also. It should be noted that bankers may prefer to use profit after tax in calculating this ratio. Remember, therefore, the importance of knowing what fig-ures are used if you expect to compare ratios from different sources.

If you save money at the building society or have investments in quoted companies, you will be interested in the return that you make on your money. This is usually expressed as a percentage of the amount invested, say, 10 per cent. In the same way, profitability ratios show how good your business is as an investment. Furthermore, both lenders and third-party investors will want to know the overall return on capital, as an indication of the security of the investment as well as an indicator of how well the business is performing, by giving a comparison with what could have been achieved had the same sum of money been saved or invested on the stock market. Accountants and banks, depending on their preferences, may look at:

- Return on equity (RoE)
- Return on capital employed (RoCE)
- Return on invested capital (RoIC)
- Return on total assets (RoTA)

While these are all slightly different ratios they are all, in some way, looking at the return on assets. It is important, however, to be clear which figures are being used to derive the ratio and to be consistent, otherwise comparisons will be meaningless. Personally, I prefer RoCE and RoE. (In calculating ratios where one of the figures is a balance sheet item, you should use the average for the period covered by the profit and loss account. Published accounts always show the previous period's figures for comparisons. If for any reason, this is not possible, using the figure on the available balance sheet will give an approximation.)

$$RoCE = \frac{PBIT}{CE} \times 100\%$$

Capital employed (CE) was defined on page 40. Remember that I suggest that capital employed is defined to cover all loan finance.[2] Some financiers prefer to look at return on total assets (TA). (If you define capital employed as suggested above, total assets is equal to capital employed plus trade debtors plus stock.)

$$RoTA = \frac{PBIT}{TA} \times 100\%$$

[2] This definition is consistent with that used by Datastream, a major provider of company financial information in the UK.

Understanding the figures

The return to the owners can be determined by looking at the return on equity (RoE). RoE gives the owners the opportunity to compare their return with what they might achieve if they invested their money elsewhere,[3] so it is normal, to use profit after tax (PAT).

$$RoE = \frac{PAT}{NW} \times 100\%$$

We can apply the alternative methods suggested above to Young & Co's profit and loss account illustrated in Figure 4.1.

$$Gross\ profit\ margin = \frac{Gross\ profit}{Sales} \times 100\% = \frac{49,600}{72,300} \times 100\% = 69\%$$

$$Net\ profit\ margin = \frac{PBIT}{Sales} \times 100\% = \frac{7,900}{72,300} \times 100\% = 11\%$$

Note that capital employed is equal to equity (116,800) plus long-term liabilities (32,300) plus (as suggested above) short-term loans (3,400), which gives 152,500, so

$$RoCE = \frac{PBIT}{CE} \times 100\% = \frac{7,900}{152,500} \times 100\% = 5\%$$

$$RoE = \frac{PAT}{NW} \times 100\% = \frac{3,500}{116,800} \times 100\% = 3\%$$

If you do not know the tax position, or if you want to relate RoE to other ratios of return on capital, you could use PBIT instead of PAT.

EXERCISE

Katie's Kitchen – Profitability

Look at the profit and loss account and balance sheet figures that you have already calculated for Katie's Kitchens. Now calculate

- Gross profit margin
- Net profit margin
- Return on capital employed
- Return on equity

---

[3] Note that Datastream adds deferred tax and subtracts intangible assets from the net worth figure in calculating RoE.

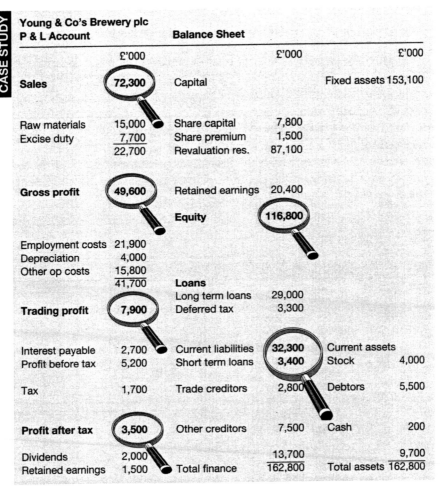

Figure 4.1 Balance sheet (1)

Solvency

If the net worth of the business becomes negative, that is the total liabilities exceed total assets, then the business has become insolvent. In other words, if the business closed it would not be possible to repay all the people who are owed money. Allowing a company to become insolvent is an offence, so you should take care to watch the figures closely.

One ratio which gives an indication of solvency is the *gearing*. Many businesses, as they grow larger, do choose to set a gearing objective. Gearing is normally defined as the ratio of debt (i.e. loans from all sources including debentures, term loans and overdraft) to the capital employed. The higher the proportion of loan finance, the higher the gearing.

51

$$Gearing = \frac{total\ borrowing}{equity + total\ borrowing}$$

Ideally, the gearing should not be greater than 50 per cent although it often is, particularly for new, small businesses. If cash flow is stable and profit is fairly stable, then you can afford a higher gearing. It may be worth noting that banks frequently include the overdraft facility rather than the actual level of overdraft being used when they calculate gearing.

You may also come across the term *leverage* which is just a different way of defining the gearing of the business. Leverage is defined as the capital employed divided by the equity.

Effect of gearing

The gearing of a business can have an important effect on the return achieved on capital. The only way to improve the efficiency with which you use your capital is to make it work harder for you.

This is more difficult than it sounds. One way is to employ less equity in the business and to use more loan finance. Let us look at a simple example.

Ignoring the effect of taxation, Company A has £20,000 capital employed, all of which is equity and makes a profit of £5,000. RoCE is, therefore, 25 per cent. RoE is also 25 per cent. Company B has £20,000 capital employed; half is equity and half is borrowed from the bank at 12½ per cent. It, too, makes a profit of £5,000 so RoCE is still 25 per cent. Interest reduces the profit to £3,750 giving an RoE of 38 per cent, dramatically higher than Company A.

Company C also has £20,000 capital employed, but in this case just £2,000 is equity and £18,000 is borrowed, again at 12½ per cent. Its profit of £5,000 still gives an RoCE of 25 per cent. Interest reduces the profit to £2,750 but this is now a substantial 138 per cent RoE.

If the RoCE falls below the cost of borrowing money then the leverage works in the other direction. Company D has £20,000 capital employed all of which is equity. It makes a profit of £2,000 and, therefore, an RoCE of 10 per cent.

Company E has £20,000 capital employed of which half is a loan at 12½ per cent. Profit before interest of £2,000 is reduced to £750 after interest of £1,250 is deducted to give an RoE of 8 per cent.

Company F has £20,000 capital employed of which £18,000 is a loan at 12½ per cent. It makes a profit of £2,000 also giving an RoCE of 10 per cent, but it is in real trouble. Its interest amounts to £2,250 giving an overall loss of £250. As a result equity investors, who will not have to contribute to losses, will want gearing as high as possible to benefit from the leverage effect of a RoCE higher than the cost of borrowing money. Conversely lenders, worried about the opposite leverage effect and the ability of a business to pay its interest charges, will want the gearing as low as possible.

In addition to watching the gearing, bankers will also want to be satisfied that you will be able to pay the interest on their loans. They particularly look, therefore, at how many times your profit exceeds their interest.

$$Interest\ cover = \frac{Profit\ before\ interest\ and\ tax}{Interest}$$

If this is more than 4 it is very good. If it is less than 2 it may indicate potential problems if interest rates rise. We can use Young & Co's figures once again (Figure 4.2) to illustrate these points.

$$Gearing = \frac{Loans}{CE} \times 100\% = \frac{35,700}{152,500} \times 100\% = 23\%$$

53

Although capital employed is a balance sheet figure, it is the gearing at a specific time that is important. You should, therefore, simply take the equity and debt figures from the most recent balance sheet and not the average for the period.

$$Interest\ cover = \frac{PBIT}{Interest} = \frac{7,900}{2,700} = 2.9\ times$$

Katie's Kitchens – Solvency

EXERCISE

For Katie's Kitchens, calculate
- Gearing
- Interest cover

Liquidity ratios

A business should always have enough current assets (e.g. stock, work in progress, debtors, cash in the bank and so on) to cover current liabilities (e.g. bank overdraft, creditors and so on). Liquidity ratios indicate the ability of the business to meet liabilities with the assets available. The current ratio shows the relationship of current assets to current liabilities.

Young & Co's Brewery plc
P & L Account   **Balance Sheet**

	£'000		£'000		£'000
Sales	72,300	Capital		Fixed assets	153,100
Raw materials	15,000	Share capital	7,800		
Excise duty	7,700	Share premium	1,500		
	22,700	Revaluation res.	87,100		
Gross profit	49,600	Retained earnings	20,400		
		Equity	**116,800**		
Employment costs	21,900				
Depreciation	4,000				
Other op costs	15,800				
	41,700	**Loans**			
		Long term loans	29,000		
Trading profit	**7,900**	Deferred tax	3,300		
Interest payable	**2,700**	Current liabilities	**32,300**	Current assets	
		Short term loans	**3,400**	Stock	4,000
Profit before tax	5,200				
Tax	1,700	Trade creditors	2,800	Debtors	5,500
Profit after tax	3,500	Other creditors	7,500	Cash	200
Dividends	2,000		13,700		9,700
Retained earnings	1,500	Total finance	162,800	Total assets	162,800

Figure 4.2   Balance sheet (2)

$$Current\ ratio = \frac{Current\ assets}{Current\ liabilities}$$

This ratio should normally be between 1.5 and 2. Some people argue that the current ratio should be at least 2 on the basis that half the assets might be stock. If it is less than 1 (i.e. current liabilities exceed current assets) you could be insolvent. A stricter test of liquidity is the quick ratio or acid test. Some current assets, such as work in progress and stock, can be difficult to turn quickly into cash. Deducting these from the current assets gives the quick assets.

$$Quick\ ratio = \frac{Quick\ assets}{Current\ liabilities}$$

The quick ratio should normally be around 0.7–1. To be absolutely safe, the quick ratio should be at least 1, which indicates that quick assets exceed current liabilities. If the current ratio is rising and the quick ratio is static, there is almost certainly a stockholding problem. You need to counteract this by selling off your excess stock. If you can't, you need to review whether customers want to buy your product at the price at which you are trying to sell.

Some people and banks in particular find it helpful to calculate the 'defensive interval'. This is the best measure of impending insolvency and shows the number of days the business can exist if no more cash flows into the business. As a guide, it should be 30–90 days, though it is industry prone. The daily operating expenses are best determined from the cash flow statement – take the total payments for the year and divide by 365. If a cash flow figure is not easily available, you can make an approximation by taking figures from the profit and loss account – take total payments, add interest and deduct depreciation – and make a stab at adding net loan repayments estimated from the balance sheet.

55

$$Defensive\ interval\ (days) = \frac{Quick\ assets}{daily\ operating\ expenses}$$

$$Current\ ratio = \frac{current\ assets}{current\ liabilities} = \frac{9,700}{13,700} = 0.7$$

$$Quick\ ratio = \frac{quick\ assets}{current\ liabilities} = \frac{5,700}{13,700} = 0.4$$

$$Defensive\ interval = \frac{quick\ assets}{daily\ operating\ expenses} = \frac{5,700}{63,100/365} = 33\ days$$

(Note that daily operating expenses has been estimated here as cost of sales (£22,700) plus overheads (£41,700) less depreciation (£4,000) plus interest (£2,700).)

EXERCISE

Katie's Kitchens – Liquidity

For Katie's Kitchens, calculate
- Current ratio
- Quick ratio
- Defensive interval

Young & Co's Brewery plc

P & L Account		Balance Sheet		
	£'000		£'000	£'000
Sales	72,300	Capital		Fixed assets 153,100
Raw materials	15,000	Share capital	7,800	
Excise duty	7,700	Share premium	1,500	
Cost of sales	22,700	Revaluation res.	87,100	
Gross profit	49,600	Retained earnings	20,400	
		Equity	116,800	
Employment costs	21,900			
Depreciation	4,000			
Other op costs	15,800			
	41,700	Loans		
		Long term loans	29,000	
Trading profit	7,900	Deferred tax	3,300	
Interest payable	2,700	Current liabilities	32,300	Current assets
		Short term loans	3.400	Stock 4,000
Profit before tax	5,200			
Tax	1,700	Trade creditors	2,800	Debtors 5,500
Profit after tax	3,500	Other creditors	7,500	Cash 200
Dividends	2,000		13,700	9,700
Retained earnings	1,500	Total finance	162,800	Total assets 162,800

Figure 4.3   Balance sheet (3)

Efficiency ratios

Efficiency ratios provide a measure of how much working capital is tied up, indicate how quickly you collect outstanding debts and pay your creditors and show how effective you are in making your money work for you. They also indicate the management efficiency of the business. You will be particularly keen to monitor how quickly your debtors pay you.

$$Debtors'\ turnover\ ratio = \frac{sales}{average\ debtors\ (ex\ VAT)}$$

Ideally use the average debtors for the period. An approximation is given by dividing the sales by the debtors at the end of the period. Dividing this ratio into the days of the year gives the average collection period in days.

$$Average\ collection\ period = \frac{365 \times debtors\ (ex\ VAT)}{sales}$$

Tight credit control is essential. Keep the collection period as short as possible. Many businesses aim to operate on 30 days, but often find it is worse than that.

Monitoring how long it takes to pay your suppliers is as important as knowing how long your customers take to pay you. If suppliers have to wait too long, they may withdraw credit facilities.

$$Creditors'\ turnover\ ratio = \frac{cost\ of\ sales}{average\ creditors\ (ex\ VAT)}$$

$$Average\ payment\ period = \frac{365 \times creditors\ (ex\ VAT)}{cost\ of\ sales}$$

It is normal to use cost of sales in calculating the average payment period when comparing your business with others. However, you may need to approximate by using the sales figures unless you can determine the cost of sales of your competitors.

Stock will increase in time of expansion and decrease in times of contraction. For some businesses, such as wholesalers and some retailers, a high stock turnover ratio is essential in order to make any profit. A low stock turnover could indicate the presence of slow moving stock, which may be a problem that you will need to address.

$$Stock\ turnover\ ratio = \frac{cost\ of\ sales}{average\ stock}$$

It is often helpful to know the stock holding period.

$$Average\ stock\ holding\ period = \frac{365 \times stock}{cost\ of\ sales}$$

A fruit shop, for example, would expect an average holding period of no more than a couple of days, otherwise the fruit will deteriorate and sales will be lost. A bookshop, on the other hand, might have a stock turn of just 3–4 and a holding period of around 90–120 days. This is because it needs to carry a very high level of stock in order to give sufficient choice to its customers. Holding stock for too long has serious implications for the amount of money that the business has tied up in stock. A measure of how hard the assets of the business are being made to work is given by the *asset turn* or *capital turnover*. Ideally, use the average total assets for the period.

$$\text{Asset turn} = \frac{Sales}{Average\ total\ assets}$$

Some accountants use net assets when calculating this ratio and some use current assets so take particular care when other people are quoting asset turn. For a large British company the asset turn is typically 1.1.[4] A profitable company would typically have an asset turn of 1.3–1.5. Note that

$$Net\ profit\ margin \times asset\ turn = ROTA$$

A net profit margin of around 10 per cent, combined with an asset turn of 1.4, would give a return on total assets of 14 per cent.

Let us look once again at Young & Co (Figure 4.4):

$$\text{Average collection period} = \frac{365 \times debtors}{Sales} = \frac{365 \times 5,500}{72,300} = 28\ \text{days}$$

$$\text{Average payment period} = \frac{365 \times creditors}{Cost\ of\ sales} = \frac{365 \times 2,800}{22,700} = 45\ \text{days}$$

$$\text{Stock holding period} = \frac{365 \times stock}{Cost\ of\ sales} = \frac{365 \times 4,000}{22,700} = 64\ \text{days}$$

$$\text{Asset turn} = \frac{Sales}{Total\ assets} = \frac{72,300}{162,800} = 0.44$$

[4] Ciaren Walsh, *Key Management Ratios*, FT/Pitman Publishing, 1993.

Young & Co's Brewery plc

P & L Account		Balance Sheet			
	£'000		£'000		£'000
Sales	72,300	Capital		Fixed assets	153,100
Raw materials	15,000	Share capital	7,800		
Excise duty	7,700	Share premium	1,500		
Cost of sales	22,700	Revaluation res.	87,100		
Gross profit	49,600	Retained earnings	20,400		
		Equity	116,800		
Employment costs	21,900				
Depreciation	4,000				
Other op costs	15,800				
	41,700	**Loans**			
		Long term loans	29,000		
Trading profit	7,900	Deferred tax	3,300		
Interest payable	2,700	Current liabilities	32,300	Current assets	
Profit before tax	5,200	Short term loans	3,400	Stock	4,000
Tax	1,700	Trade creditors	2,800	Debtors	5,500
Profit after tax	3,500	Other creditors	7,500	Cash	200
Dividends	2,000		13,700		9,700
Retained earnings	1,500	Total finance	162,800	Total assets	162,800

Figure 4.4   Balance sheet (4)

Katie's Kitchens – Efficiency

For Katie's Kitchens, calculate:

- Debtors' turnover ratio
- Average collection period
- Creditors' turnover ratio
- Average payment period
- Stock turnover ratio
- Average holding period
- Asset turnover

Keeping costs under control is absolutely essential if the net profit margin is to be maintained – or increased. It will help to consider costs both in absolute terms as well as a percentage of sales revenue. The objective should be to restrict them to a maximum percentage once again. These figures can be compared year on year and against competitors if they are turned into ratios. For example:

$$\frac{Selling\ costs}{Sales}$$

Selling costs include all marketing and advertising costs as well as the payroll costs of any sales people that you employ. They might also include distribution costs. Are the selling costs being contained? Is the effort put into selling reflected in the sales? Watching this figure carefully will also provide data to help in the preparation of demand curves.

$$\frac{Administration\ costs}{Sales}$$

Are the administration costs being maintained? If they are very low, is customer service suffering?

$$\frac{Production\ costs}{Sales}$$

Production costs include raw material costs, costs of any sub-contract work, labour costs involved in the production process and any overheads directly associated with the production process. For most small businesses, production costs will simply be raw materials and sub-contract work, that is, direct costs. It is very difficult to control overheads. Left unchallenged, they will grow and eat into profits. Use ratios such as these to watch for sudden increases or variances. But also continually look to see if there are ways to reduce the total overhead burden.

Relationships between ratios

As you might expect, all these ratios can be related to one another, building up into a ratio tree. (see Figure 4.5). The ratios on the left-hand side are concerned with profitability and cost ratios; those on the right-hand side cover the liquidity and efficiency of the business.

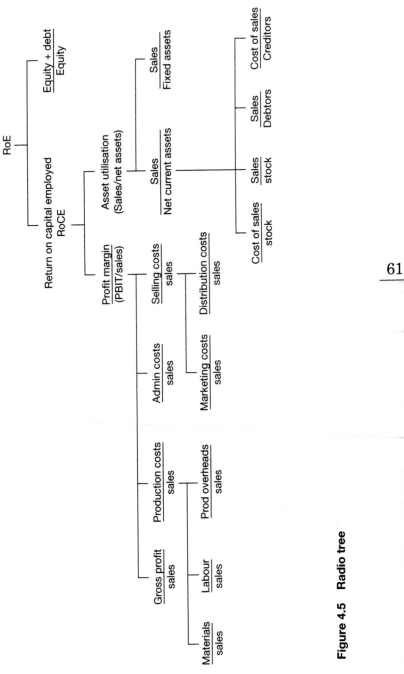

Figure 4.5 Radio tree

Staff performance

Many businesses use ratios which show the overall performance of the business using the number of staff as the denominator rather than a monetary figure. Some common performance indicators are

$$Profit\ per\ employee = \frac{PBIT}{Number\ of\ employees}$$

$$Output\ per\ employee = \frac{Sales}{Number\ of\ employees}$$

Compaq, for example, boasts that its sales in 1993 were equal to £450,000 per employee, up from £190,000 in 1991. Nintendo, in 1992, did even better. Its 892 employees achieved sales of £3.5bn and pretax profits of £800m. That's equivalent to sales of £3.8m/employee and profit of £1.5m/employee.

It may also be helpful to look at a measure of productivity which relates employment costs to sales.

$$Productivity = \frac{Sales}{Employment\ costs}$$

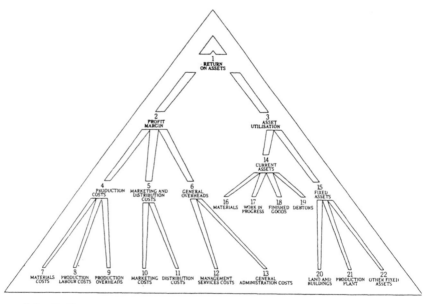

Figure 4.6   Ratio tree

(*Source:* Centre for Interim Comparison)

Industry averages

It is possible in many industries to discover the typical ratios for the sector. You could acquire the annual reports of a number of companies and calculate them for yourself, or else you can buy reports from the Centre for Interfirm Comparison (CIFC) or from ICC Business Publications Ltd.

CIFC are commissioned by businesses, or sometimes by trade associations, to review typical ratios for a particular sector. Ratios can be grouped together into trees which show how the ratios interrelate. Typically, CIFC would agree those ratios to be reviewed and group them into a tree as shown in Figure 4.6. Note the similarity with the tree in the previous figure. They then produce tables showing the performance of companies within the sector and also calculate industry averages, as shown in Figure 4.7.

TABLE 1 OF 10		*Firms*												
Ratio		A	B	C	D	E	F	G	H	I	J	HIGH	AVERAGE	LOW
1. Return on Assets	%	25.2	23.9	20.1	19.0	14.7	13.8	12.3	6.7	5.3	4.3	25.2	14.5	4.3
Profit margin on sales and turnover of assets														
2. Profit margin	%	13.1	14.8	13.5	11.7	10.3	9.1	7.7	3.7	3.1	2.9	14.8	9.0	2.9
3. Asset utilisation	times p.a.	1.92	1.61	1.49	1.62	1.43	1.52	1.60	1.81	1.70	1.48	1.92	1.62	1.43
Total costs as a % of sales														
4. Production costs	%	64.5	64.7	65.5	69.1	73.4	68.4	78.4	79.2	81.1	80.1	81.1	72.8	65.5
5. Marketing and distribution costs	%	15.6	13.8	15.9	14.7	11.6	16.3	8.6	11.6	12.1	12.0	16.3	13.2	8.6
6. General overheads	%	4.8	4.7	5.1	4.5	4.7	6.2	5.3	5.5	3.7	5.0	6.2	5.0	3.7
Ratio 2 above	%	13.1	14.8	13.5	11.7	10.3	9.1	7.7	3.7	3.1	2.9	14.8	9.0	2.9
	%	100.0	100.0	100.0	100.0	100.0	100.0	100.0	100.0	100.0	100.0		100.0	
Production costs as a % of sales value of production														
7. Materials costs	%	47.9	44.6	45.7	48.7	46.3	46.6	49.1	52.1	50.3	49.9	52.1	48.1	44.6
8. Production labour costs	%	10.6	11.1	12.1	12.4	13.5	13.3	13.8	14.1	17.7	14.6	17.7	13.3	10.6
9. Production overheads	%	8.0	11.0	7.7	8.0	13.6	8.5	15.5	13.0	13.1	15.6	15.6	11.4	7.7
Ratio 4 above	%	64.5	64.7	65.5	69.1	73.4	68.4	78.4	79.2	81.1	80.1	81.1	72.8	65.5
Marketing and distribution costs as a % of sales														
10. Marketing costs	%	10.0	9.5	10.7	9.5	7.4	10.1	4.0	7.4	4.8	6.2	10.7	7.9	4.0
11. Distribution costs	%	5.6	4.3	5.2	5.2	4.2	6.2	4.6	4.2	7.3	5.8	7.3	5.3	4.2
Ratio 5 above	%	15.6	13.8	15.9	14.7	11.6	16.3	8.6	11.6	12.1	12.0	16.3	13.2	8.6
General and administration costs as a % of sales														
12. Management services costs	%	1.6	1.7	2.0	1.2	1.4	1.6	1.2	1.2	1.3	1.1	2.0	1.5	1.1
13. General administration costs	%	3.2	3.0	3.1	3.3	3.3	4.6	4.1	4.3	2.4	3.9	4.6	3.5	2.4
Ratio 6 above	%	4.8	4.7	5.1	4.5	4.7	6.2	5.3	5.5	3.7	5.0	6.2	5.0	3.7
Value of assets in £s per £1,000 of sales														
14. Current assets	%	199	242	251	242	309	286	245	187	240	273	309	248	187
15. Fixed assets	%	322	379	420	375	390	370	380	365	348	403	420	375	322
Total assets	%	521	621	671	617	699	656	625	552	588	676	699	623	521
Current assets in £s per £1,000 of sales														
16. Materials	%	61	77	75	73	134	86	60	50	65	62	134	74	50
17. Work in progress	%	7	7	10	8	9	12	10	8	15	12	15	10	7
18. Finished goods	%	11	10	15	11	11	18	15	14	15	17	18	14	10
19. Debtors	%	120	148	151	150	155	170	160	115	145	182	182	150	115
Ratio 14 above	%	199	242	251	242	309	286	245	187	240	273	309	248	187
Fixed assets in £s per £1,000 of sales														
20. Land and buildings	%	187	210	255	211	210	205	191	202	164	180	255	202	164
21. Production plant	%	118	129	145	146	148	141	168	144	150	182	182	147	118
22. Other fixed assets	%	17	40	20	18	32	24	21	19	30	41	41	26	17
Ratio 15 above	%	322	379	420	375	390	370	380	365	344	403	420	375	322

ASSETS | PRODUCTIVITY | GROWTH

Figure 4.7 Industry ratio averages
(*Source:* Centre for Interfirm Comparison)

The two figures show typical ratios for use by a business in the manufacturing sector. CIFC also apply the same principles, but use different ratios, for businesses in service sectors and also in the public and not for profit sectors. For a professional firm, such as solicitors, CIFC might start with, say, profit per partner. For a distribution business, they might isolate different costs to generate, say, cost per mile or cost per tonne. In all cases, the overall objectives are

- to provide comparisons with the performance of other businesses in a similar field, and
- to provide an appropriate set of ratios which individual businesses can use to improve their own control.

If you cannot afford a CIFC report or there is not one available for your industry then look for ICC Business Ratios, often available from your local library. They produce reports looking at specific markets and provide a considerable amount of information on companies in the sector under review. They also publish Regional Company Surveys which give more limited information about more businesses.

Value added analysis

64

The price of the products (or service) that you sell equals the costs of the raw materials or services bought in plus the value that you have added. This *added value* equals the proportion of overhead costs attributed together with your profit. Note that the overhead costs in value added calculations are not the same as the fixed costs. The bulk of fixed cost items are, in fact, bought in, but the major element of added value is the work input by you and your staff. The sales price of your product (or service) represents its value to your customers. The value added represents the amount by which your business has contributed to the creation of the country's wealth. That contribution is shared between four parties: the owners, the employees, reinvestment and the government (through taxes). A profit and loss account concentrates solely on the level of profit and is aimed at shareholders. A value added statement concentrates on the wealth creation and shows its distribution.

Added value can be used as a measure of efficiency. For example, value added per employee is sometimes used to measure the efficiency of labour. The ratio of value added to wages gives a measure of staff productivity. The ratio value added to capital employed gives an indication of capital productivity.

Published value added statements are still quite rare, though they are easy to calculate from published accounts. Some companies use them to demonstrate how large a proportion of their income goes to their employees and the government and how little to shareholders.

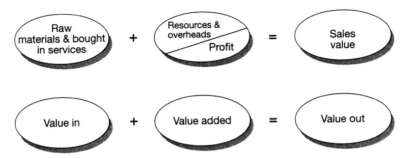

Figure 4.8   Added value

There are two methods of calculating the value added by a business, both of which, of course, should give the same answer. These are the subtraction method and the addition method. In the subtraction method, all the raw material and bought-in service costs are deducted from the total sales. In the addition method, the employment costs, interest, dividend payments, tax, depreciation and retained profit are added together. Look back at the profit and loss account for Young & Co's Brewery. Calculate their added value. Now look at the figure below. Young's have around 1,580 employees, so each employee has added value of £26,000.

CASE STUDY	Young & Co's Brewery plc Added value	£'000	%
	Subtraction method		
	Sales during year	72,300	100
	less: Raw materials etc.	15,000	21
	All services bought in	15,800	22
	Value added	41,500	57
	Addition method		
	Employment costs	21,900	53
	Interest	2,700	7
	Dividends & profit share	2,000	5
	Tax	1,700	3
	Beer duty	7,700	19
	Depreciation	4,000	10
	Profit retained	1,500	3
	Value added	41,500	100
	Number of employees (FTE)	1,580	
	Value added per employee	26	

As can be seen from the example, half the added value goes in employment costs and a further 22 per cent goes to the government. Value added analysis can be used on a customer by customer basis. In a sense this is the same as looking at the gross profit on each job. If fixed overheads are being allocated fairly, it is very easy to see the level of net profit on each job – and perhaps to decide whether to take on a particular contract. For example, you may be more willing to under-take a job at a finer net profit margin for a regular customer than you would be for a one off enquirer.

Choosing appropriate objectives

When you consider your strategic objectives and your annual business plan, you will want to define the objectives in financial terms (as well as marketing, quality and people terms). If, as suggested in Chapter 2, a key objective is to make money, then it is essential that one of your targets defines return on capital. If you are in manufacturing, then you are likely to have an investment in capital that is high compared to sales turnover (and, in consequence, a low asset turn). You will proba-bly want to set a target for return on equity. If part of the reason that you are in business is to create a job for yourself, or because you do not want to work for someone else, it is unlikely that you will be discour-aged by a low return on your investment. It probably makes more sense, in that instance, to monitor the return on capital employed, which clearly needs to be greater than the cost of your loan. Achieving this will provide you with good ammunition when you are negotiating with potential lenders or investors. Achieving your desired RoCE is a long-term, or strategic, objective.

Service businesses are not as likely to have so much capital tied up in fixed assets, though increasingly service businesses do find that they need heavy investment in information technology. They may also have capital tied up in premises. If you run a service business, you may think that it makes more sense to use staff performance ratios rather than profitability ratios (such as sales per employee and net profit per employee) rather than profitability ratios based on capital returns.

To achieve the desired return you will need a target for net profit, so you will also want to set and monitor sales targets closely and ensure that you are achieving both the volume and the value targets. Achiev-ing these targets, and keeping costs within their targets, will ensure that you achieve the return on capital or the staff performance targets that you have set. In setting financial objectives, you are committing yourself to perform to a certain standard. Monitoring the ratios suggested is straightforward if you have a computerised accounting package – though identifying what corrective action to take if the actual results differ from the targets may not be so clear.

Simply setting targets is insufficient by itself. You will also need to prepare financial forecasts which show how you might achieve those targets – and some may need time to achieve. You might decide, for example, to set a target of 15 per cent return on capital employed by the end of the third year from now. However, that might require an annual increase of gross profit of 10 per cent which, in turn, might require an annual increase in sales of, say, 20 per cent.

Conclusion and checklist

Using ratios to set targets and then to monitor performance will assist you to know, at all times, the financial position of your business. Ratios can be used to monitor whether you are on target in relation to sales as well as in keeping control of costs. They can also be useful in making comparisons with competitors and your own previous performance. Not every business will wish to use all the ratios explained in this chapter, though all will benefit from keeping a close eye on

- gross profit margin
- net profit margin

If the business achieves these, it will almost certainly keep within its cost targets and achieve its return on capital targets. Monitoring payment days, collection days and stock turn will help you keep an eye on working capital requirements which, in turn, will keep you within your borrowing limits.

The previous two chapters have assumed that there are figures to interpret. This requires the business to generate sales, to ensure that it costs its activities carefully and sets an appropriate price and that it has a plan which is realistic and achievable. These are the topics of the next part of the book.

67

Part 3

.

Planning for profit

5

Costing and pricing

- **The price charged for a product or service depends on what the market will stand, i.e. what the customer will pay.**
- **The cost of producing that product or service depends on the business's ability to keep all its costs under control.**
- **The difference between price and cost is profit – or loss!**
- **Profit also depends on your ability to sell enough product or service, so knowing the break even point and monitoring progress towards it may be helpful.**

Many people have some difficulty calculating the cost of their products or services and, as a result, let their competitors effectively set the price. As mentioned earlier, however, profit is the relatively small difference between the two relatively large numbers of sales revenue and expenditure. A small change in one of those can cause a large change in profit, so getting both price and cost right is clearly important.

Elements of pricing

You need to charge a price that will cover all your costs and generate a reasonable profit. Remember that there is little relationship between costing and pricing. The price should be the maximum amount that people will pay for your product or service. The cost is the cost to you of making the product or delivering the service, although it is not always immediately clear how to calculate the costs. Costing methods aim to allocate costs between jobs and periods. In addition, however, your objectives should always include attempts to reduce costs and to improve productivity. Keeping the price high and the costs low will, therefore, maximise profit. But you need to know how to spread the costs. If you are manufacturing, how do you spread the costs over the total number of items? If you make a range of products how do you allocate costs across products? If you are offering a service, how do you spread the costs over the total number of hours of service?

Defining costs

It is easy to see all the different costs that a business incurs, but it is often helpful to divide these up. You may have heard people talk about direct and indirect costs, fixed and variable costs. Some of these terms are used interchangeably although they should not be.

As described in Chapter 3 direct costs are those that can be directly attributed (and are usually measurable) to the production of a particular product or service. Raw materials are direct costs. Sub-contracting is a direct cost. Deducting the direct costs from the sales revenue for a particular product gives its contribution towards overheads and profit.

Variable costs are those that vary in proportion to the level of production. These will include, for example, raw materials, direct labour and sub-contract work. However, some overhead costs, such as use of electricity, may also vary with total production even though they are difficult to allocate directly. Variable costs are sometimes called marginal costs by accountants.

Fixed costs, on the other hand, do not vary in the short term and are not dependent on the level of production. These include, for example, rent, rates, insurance and managers' salaries.

Indirect costs are the opposite of direct costs – those costs that cannot be directly attributed to a specific product. It can be seen that fixed costs are indirect; variable costs, though, might be direct or indirect. Most small businesses do not need to worry too much about these definitions. The overheads are indirect: some will vary with the level of production; some will be fixed. For most small businesses, the overheads can generally be regarded as fixed, at least in the short term. If you are self-employed (as a sole trader or a partner) the money available to you is the profit, that is, the sales revenue less all the costs. Naturally, you need to draw money out from the business on a regular basis, but those drawings are simply an advance against profit. Furthermore, you are taxed on the entire profit. For the purpose of calculating costs, therefore, it probably makes sense to treat your drawings and any income tax as an overhead cost. All too frequently, sole proprietors and partners forget to include their drawings and tax when calculating costs.

If you run a limited company, then your salary is regarded as a business overhead and you will be paying tax through the PAYE scheme. It should be included as an expense along with all other staff costs. The only extra tax will be corporation tax which is charged on the net profit.

Manufacturing cost

If you are manufacturing, you can calculate the cost per item by:

$$Item\ cost = \frac{Overheads}{Total\ items} + Direct\ cost\ per\ item$$

Dividing the total overheads by the number of items you expect to sell spreads the overheads. Adding any direct costs gives the total cost for the item.

Imagine that you make desks. You have estimated your total overheads for the year as £30,000 including depreciation, drawings and tax. You expect to make and sell 100 desks during the year. The cost of wood and other materials for each desk is £50. The cost is calculated as follows:

$$Desk\ cost = \frac{30,000}{100} + 50 = £350$$

You then need to add a profit margin, say 10 per cent, and VAT at 17½ per cent if you are registered for VAT. This gives a selling price of £452.

Service based businesses

If you provide a service, such as industrial design or writing bespoke software, you will need to know how much to charge per hour, though you may estimate the total time required and offer your customers a fixed price when quoting. This can be expressed by:

$$Hourly\ rate = \frac{Overheads}{Annual\ productive\ hours}$$

Remember that not all working hours will be productive. Some time will be required for promoting your business, buying supplies, doing the books etc. You will need some holidays and you should also allow for possible illness.

Imagine that you are a photographer. As above, your total overheads for the year are £30,000. After allowing for holidays and illness you estimate that you will be able to sell 200 days of your time. You expect to average 7½ hours per day. Thus:

$$Hourly\ rate = \frac{30,000}{1,500} = £20\ per\ hour$$

73

As with manufactured items you need to add the direct costs (film, developing, printing etc.), profit margin and VAT. For a one-day assignment you will charge time (£150) + direct costs (say £40) + profit (say 20 per cent) + VAT (17½ per cent) giving a total price of £268.

Decor by Diane

Imagine that you are the owner of a painting and decorating business. You employ five staff in addition to yourself. You expect to undertake 240 jobs next year at an average of six days per job. Each of your staff costs you £15,000 per annum (including NI). Your overhead costs are £24,000 per annum. You hope to draw at least £20,000 net from the business. How much would you expect to charge for the average job? Remember to consider the implications of tax and the need to make a profit.

Retail businesses

Some businesses are simply engaged in buying and selling; many of those, particularly retailers, have an extremely wide range of products. They tend to think about the *mark up* required to cover their overheads. The mark up is simply the inverse of the gross profit margin. If you buy clothes to sell in your shop, you may want to choose to mark up the price by 100 per cent. In other words, you sell everything for twice what you paid for it. This gives a gross profit margin of 50 per cent. People often confuse margin and mark up so take care. For example, a 50 per cent mark up on cost equals 33⅓ per cent gross profit on sales.

You need to estimate your likely total sales and to know *all* your overhead costs. Your margin must still cover all your overhead costs, otherwise you will not make any profit. And you still need to keep your costs under control.

Allocating overheads

If you make more than one product, you need to split the business overheads between the different products. There are a number of ways in which you may choose to divide the fixed overheads; on the basis of the volume manufactured of each different product, or the time taken to make each product, or the floor area needed by each production process, or pro rata according to the sales income of each product. It may be appropriate to use a combination. For example, imagine that you run a business manufacturing three products. Sales and costs are as shown:

	One	Two	Three	Total
Sales	10,000	20,000	15,000	45,000
Direct costs	5,000	10,000	10,000	25,000
Fixed costs	4,000	8,000	6,000	18,000
Total costs	9,000	18,000	16,000	43,000
Net profit	1,000	2,000	(1,000)	2,000

The fixed costs are split up between the three in proportion to total sales income, i.e. 40 per cent. As can be seen, product three is apparently making a loss. Should you stop manufacturing this product? Even if you do, the fixed costs will generally remain the same so you will still have to recover £18,000. Let's look at the figures in a different way.

	One	Two	Three	Total
Sales	10,000	20,000	15,000	45,000
Direct costs	5,000	10,000	10,000	25,000
Contribution	5,000	10,000	5,000	20,000
Fixed costs				18,000
Net profit				2,000

If you look at the contribution of each product, you can see that all the products do make a contribution. The total contribution is £20,000 which covers the total fixed costs and leaves a net profit of £2,000. Stopping production of product three would cut £5,000 contribution leaving only £15,000 total contribution and a loss of £3,000. In this particular case, there may be a more accurate way of splitting the fixed costs in order to set a reasonably accurate price for each product. Rent and rates might be split according to floor area required; advertising might be split pro rata on sales value; product liability insurance might be split pro rata on sales volume, etc.

You might be able to think of all your products as multiples of a basic product. One joinery firm, for example, splits its fixed costs by regarding everything as chairs. Obviously a chair equals a chair. But a table was equal to three chairs, a wardrobe was equal to six chairs, etc. Market research suggested how many of each item might be sold and the fixed costs were allocated accordingly.

Whichever method used will be arbitrary – arguments can be made for and against any method of allocating fixed or indirect costs.

How do you derive the total cost?

Once you have determined how to allocate the overhead costs per item or per hour, you are then ready to add the direct costs to give the total cost. Adding an additional profit margin and VAT, if appropriate, provides you with the sales price. You will, of course, have to compare your price with the competition. If it is higher, do you offer a better quality? If it is lower, are you aiming to position yourself lower in the marketplace or could you sell at a higher price and make more profit? If your product is new, or unique, then you might be able to set your price higher, reducing it later when competitors appear.

EXAMPLE

Graham's Graphics

How should Graham Watts of Graham's Graphics decide how much to charge customers? He could use several approaches, such as the going rate for commercial designers, or charge the most possible while still being cheap enough to attract customers. On one-off contracts how would he know how much to charge? Each one will be different requiring different material, etc. However, the main problem is how much to charge for one hour of Graham's time. How valuable is he? He must charge enough per hour to ensure he makes a profit.

How could you begin to come to a reasonable figure? From your budget, you have isolated your overheads, i.e. rent, rates, etc. – costs that will be incurred whether work is being done or not. The price Graham needs to charge will be equal to:

$$\frac{Fixed\ costs + Annual\ drawings}{Annual\ productive\ hours} + Direct\ costs + Material\ costs + Profit\ margin$$

If the business is VAT registered then a further 17.5 per cent would need to be added to the price and if Graham Watts is the only person working for the firm the business time he charges to jobs in the year must cover all the overheads that the business incurs.

Overheads for the year	
Rent	4,800
Rates	1,200
Service charge	800
Car expenses	1,200
Telephone	1,000
Other	1,200
Depreciation	2,000
	12,200

Graham wishes to take out of the business £20,000 to cover his own personal costs. Therefore, Graham Watts needs to recover £32,200 by charging out his labour.

He expects to work 47 weeks each year, allowing for four weeks' holidays and one week's illness. He knows he will also have to spend at least one hour each day on average dealing with the accounting records, answering telephone calls, getting new customers, etc., and his total working week is 40 hours. It is only productive hours, though, that he can charge to customers i.e. 35 hours per week. Therefore, he expects to work 1,645 hours per year (i.e. 47 weeks x 35 hours).

However, Graham Watts feels he might not have enough customers to fill all his available time. Therefore he decides it would be better if only 75 per cent of the available hours were used in calculating the charge per hour. That is, Graham believes that, on average, 25 per cent of the time he will be available to do jobs but will have no work to do. Therefore, his productive number of hours per year = 1,645 x 75% = 1,234 hours. His hourly recovery rate, therefore, will be: $\frac{32,200}{1,234} = £26.09$

For each job, Graham will estimate how long it is going to take and then quote a price incorporating a rate of £26.09 per hour which, apart from the recovery of drawings, does not include a profit element. It will also be necessary to charge materials used on the job. To ensure all material costs are fully recovered, it is normal practice to quote something like cost plus a set percentage, or 'mark up'. Graham has decided to add 10 per cent to his materials cost. Thus, if a contract is going to take six hours and involve expenditure on materials of £120 then a price to quote would be:

Time: 6 hours at 26.09	156.54
Materials (cost + 10 %)	132.00
VAT at 17.5%	50.50
Total	339.04

If Graham wants the business to grow, he will need more profit so that he has spare money to reinvest. If he is looking for £20,000 net of tax, he will have to make more profit to pay the tax bill. This means he will either have to charge more per hour, or find more work to fill some of the other hours he has available.

Price elasticity

Fixing a price is a juggling act between strategy, costing and cash flow. It is important not to charge too low a price, otherwise the income may not cover all the costs and it may be difficult to raise prices later without putting off customers.

Maximising profit does not necessarily mean selling high volumes at low profit. It may be possible to sell low volumes at high profit. Economists argue that changing the price will cause a change in demand. The sensitivity of demand to price changes is called *price elasticity*. If demand increases more than proportionately when a product price is reduced, then the demand is elastic. If it does not, it is inelastic. Businesses will be concerned about price elasticity because they want to know how many more or fewer products will be sold if they change the price.

$$Price\ elasticity = \frac{\%\ change\ in\ demand}{\%\ change\ in\ price}$$

Unless price elasticity is relatively high (i.e. close to 1) the ability to achieve sales is not too sensitive to changes in price.

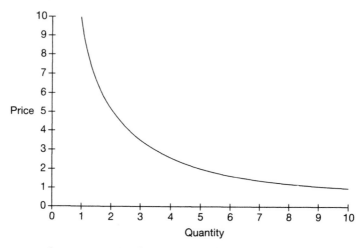

Every product or service has its own demand curve. Relating sales volume to selling price shows that the lower the price the greater the quantity sold. This can help you to think out how the change in price will affect your sales volume. It is interesting to look, for example, at the effect of price changes on the top 500 consumer brands[1]. Their price elasticity averaged 1.85. That is, each 10 per cent cut in price produced an 18.5 per cent increase in sales. However, they are all in a fiercely competitive market. It seems that market leaders tend to have a lower price elasticity so they are better supported by more advertising rather than by price promotions. Except for the market leaders, competing on price is probably the best way to increase sales of consumer products.

[1] From study by Will Hamilton of Kingston Business School reported in 'The Economist' 19 November 1994.

Cutting or raising the price may affect demand, but what will it do to overall revenue? There is also a relationship between price elasticity (E) and total revenue. If E is less than one and the price rises, revenue rises; if E is greater than one and the prices rises, revenue falls. You may find, therefore, that you cannot simply raise your prices to cover rising costs!

EXAMPLE

Perfect Prints

Nigel offers a high quality photographic service. He charges £10 for an A4 print. If he changes the price to £11, his sales drop from 1,000 units each year to 950.

$$\text{Price elasticity, } E = \frac{50/1000}{1/10} = 0.5$$

His increase in gross profit (950 units @ £1 = £950) is greater than the loss of sales income (50 @ £10 = £500).

The extra £450 is all a contribution to overheads and, once overheads are covered, to profit.

79

Pricing strategies

The greatest danger setting a price for the first time is to pitch it too low. Raising a price is always more difficult than lowering one, yet there are great temptations to undercut the competition. It is clearly important to compare your prices to your competitors', but it is essential that your price covers all your costs. There are a number of possible pricing strategies from which you might choose. These include::

- *Cost based pricing* – total costs are calculated and a mark up is added to give the required profit.
- *Skimming* – you charge a relatively high price to recover set up costs quickly if the product is good or new. As more competitors enter the market, you lower the price.
- *Individual* – you negotiate prices individually with customers based on how much they are prepared to buy.
- *Loss leaders* – if you wish to sell to a particular market then you might sell one product or service cheaper to gain market entry. You balance this by selling other products or services at a higher price. This can be risky as the danger is that everything becomes a loss leader.

- *Expected price* – what does the customer expect to pay? If you are selling a quality product, do not underprice. Often the customer expects to pay a lot as the product or service has a certain 'snob' value and this may be diminished if you underprice.
- *Differential pricing* – you charge different segments of your market different prices for the same service. For example, offering discounts to certain people like pensioners or the unemployed, or charging lower rates for quiet periods.

If, after working out your costs, the price you charge is much greater than your competitors' then you will have to look at ways of reducing costs.

Break-even analysis

Once you know your costs and estimated selling price, you are in a position to calculate how many products, or hours of your time, you need to sell to break even, that is to cover all your costs. Deducting the direct costs from the sales income gives the gross profit, also known as the contribution. Initially, it makes a contribution to covering the overheads of the business. Once all the overheads are covered, any further sales make a contribution to the profit. The easiest way to calculate the break-even point is to draw a graph. Show volume on the horizontal axis and money on the vertical axis. First show the overhead costs. This will be a horizontal line since these costs are, generally, fixed for all volumes of production.

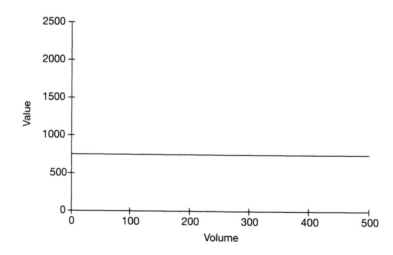

The direct costs can then be added to the overhead costs to give total costs for a given volume of output. A line representing total costs can be plotted.

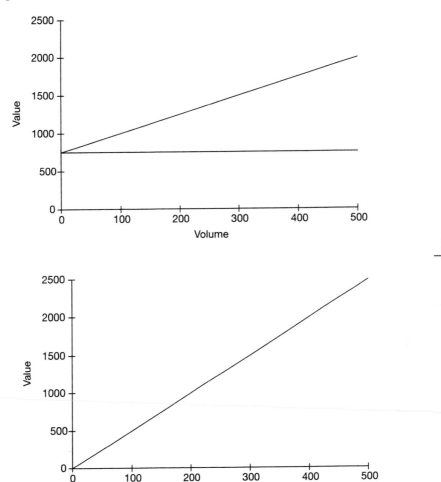

The sales income can then be plotted to show how much income will be generated for a given volume of sales. Remember that sales income starts at zero for zero sales.

These can now be combined into a single break-even chart. The point where the sales income equals the total cost shows the break-even point. A higher price will achieve break even with fewer sales. A lower price may attract more customers, but will require higher sales to break even. The further above break even that a business can operate, the greater its *margin of safety*.

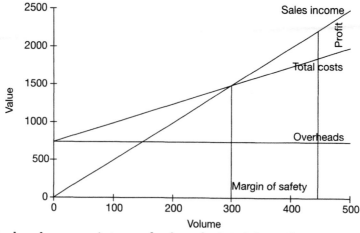

The break-even point can also be calculated from the equation:

$$BE = \frac{Fixed\ costs}{Selling\ price\ /\ unit - direct\ costs\ /\ unit}$$

All businesses should

- Keep a close eye on budgeted income and expenditure. If sales are not as high as required, you should recalculate unit cost and sales price.
- Use break-even sales volume to set monthly and annual sales figures.

It can often be helpful to plot targeted sales and actual sales on a graph in order to monitor progress regularly. If the business does not achieve its targets you will need to take remedial action.

EXERCISE

Katie's Kitchens – Costing and Break-even

While kitchen units come in a variety of shapes and sizes most are single or double floor-standing carcases and single or double wall-mounted carcases. Doors are extra. To calculate her costs and prices, Katie has decided to use a 'standard kitchen' of three floor-standing double carcases with doors and three wall-mounted double carcases with doors. All other permutations are based on this 'standard kitchen'. Katie hopes to sell 2,000 of these standard kitchens during the year. At what price does she need to sell to break even? Plot a break-even graph for Katie's Kitchens.

- What is the breakeven point?
- How great is her margin of safety?

Absorption costing

The costing method shown above has simply demonstrated one way of allocating overhead costs to your product or service. If you have more than one product or service, then as discussed earlier the difficulty arises of how the overheads should be allocated.

A slightly different way of achieving the same answer is absorption costing. In absorption costing, no distinction is made between direct and overhead costs – they are all absorbed into the cost of the product. If you make more than one product, you still have the problem of deciding how to allocate the overhead expenses across your product range. For the sake of simplicity, let us look at an example of a business that only makes one product.

EXAMPLE

Daniel's Doors

Daniel makes wooden garage doors. His overhead costs are £50,000 per annum. The direct costs, for wood and paint, are £100 per door. In absorption costing, he needs to calculate the entire costs to the business for a given level of production. If he makes 100 doors during the year, the total costs are £60,000 (i.e. £100 x 100 doors +£50,000) giving a cost per door of £600. If he makes 200 doors, the total cost is £70,000 giving a cost of £350 per door. For 500 doors the total cost is £100,000 but the cost per door has dropped to £200. Each of these are the break-even figures which can be plotted on a graph as shown below.

83

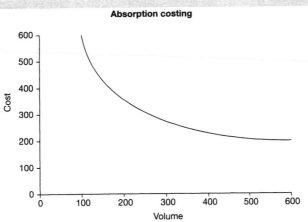

Now the break-even sales price for a given sales volume can be read from the graph. For example, if production capacity is restricted to 400 doors, then each must be sold at £225 to break even. A higher price for the same number of sales will generate a profit. Modern, computerised spreadsheet packages make production of graphs such as this simple and straightforward.

Marginal costing

The *marginal cost* of a product is the extra cost of producing one more unit. While the marginal cost is probably, for the small business, just the direct costs, it may include some overhead costs. The marginal cost can then be compared to the marginal revenue, that is, the additional contribution from one extra sale.

Clearly, the marginal cost must be set in the context of existing production. The cost of increasing production from 300 doors to 301 may be just the material costs. But if the present capacity is 400, the cost of increasing production to 401 may include new premises, new equipment, extra staff, etc. (This can be seen to affect the whole organisation and is arguably therefore a strategic decision. It will certainly also have implications for the marketing plan.)

In marginal costing, no attempt is made to allocate overhead costs to production. The contribution from each sale is simply a contribution to overheads. Once all the overheads are covered, then it becomes a contribution to profit.

EXAMPLE

Daniel's Doors

Daniel now wants to look at his costing and pricing in a different way.

	Total	Per unit
Annual sales	100,000	250
Direct and variable costs	40,000	100
Fixed costs	50,000	125
Profit	10,000	25

Assuming Daniel's estimate of sales of 400 doors at £250 is accurate, he can spread his fixed costs across those doors giving a cost per door of £225. The contribution per door is £150 and the marginal cost of manufacturing an extra door is £100. Once sufficient doors have been sold to cover the fixed costs, the contribution becomes a contribution to profit and any price over £100 becomes worthwhile.

Marginal costing can form the basis of your pricing policy if you have a clearly segmented market, using differential pricing. This policy involves selling products or services at a higher price until the demand at that price is met, and then selling the product or service at a lower price to a different segment of the market, so long as this covers unit cost – above that, any increase is a contribution to overheads or profit. An example of this is the common policy of hairdressers offering pensioners cheaper rates on Mondays and Tuesdays – days that are less popular with other clients.

The airlines in particular are becoming increasingly sophisticated at using marginal pricing in an effort to sell all the seats on their aircraft. As flights get close to departure, especially charter flights, more special offers appear. It is important, however, to remember that you must sell enough to cover all the overheads. If you reduce your gross margins for every customer, then you will need to sell more units.

As can be seen, the main difference between absorption costing and marginal costing is in the treatment of the fixed overheads. Absorption costing is normally preferred for manufacturing costs. It can be used to help:

- Control expenditure.
- Set a sales price.
- Value stock correctly (if the stock is revalued to take account of the added value).

Standard costing

One method of costing often used by larger manufacturers is known as *standard costing*. The standard cost is the cost of direct labour, direct costs and a suitable proportion of the variable overhead costs incurred in the production process. This involves the calculation of a standard time to produce the article and normally requires work study timing. For highly mechanised production it might be appropriate to use machine hours; otherwise use labour hours. The cost of labour for that length of time can then be deduced. The variable costs can be attributed, either split by the standard time or by volume. The direct costs, with an allowance for wastage, can then be added.

The main advantage of a costing system like this is that the requirement for a series of standards gives at least some criteria for measuring staff performance and provides data for variance analysis.

Activity based costing

You may also come across activity based costing: this is the practice of allocating costs to objects at cost (work, materials, services, etc.) by means of the activities performed in supporting or making those objects.

Manufacturing ratios

As well as looking at the financial performance of the business it may help, particularly if you are in a manufacturing business, to look at a number of other ratios. Many businesses, for example, attempt to measure manufacturing processes in terms of standard hours and standard costs. Detailed time and motion studies will provide an assessment of how long a particular process typically takes. A standard cost then follows based on an hour's labour together with an hour's worth of overhead. It is essential to know how long processes typically take if you are to estimate costs reasonably accurately and ensure therefore that you are not underpricing. You will also need this information when quoting delivery times to customers. You can then monitor, for example, your manufacturing efficiency ratio:

$$Efficiency\ ratio = \frac{standard\ hours}{actual\ hours}$$

If a window frame is expected to take a standard time of six hours to manufacture and actually takes eight hours, then the efficiency ratio is 6/8 or 0.75 (i.e. 75 per cent).

$$Activity\ ratio = \frac{actual\ standard\ hours}{budgeted\ standard\ hours}$$

This measures the activity of the business. If you are using standard hours, then knowing how many window frames you intend to make will give you an indication of the total budgeted hours. A business expects to make 50 window frames in a week. At 7½ hours per window frame, this will require 375 hours.

If the business actually works 400 standard hours, the window frame activity ratio is 400/375, that is 1.07 or 107 per cent. If there is a maximum number of hours available – one machine, say, might be available for 132 hours per week and require 12 hours maintenance (assuming round the clock activity) – this is an absolute constraint on the business.

$$Capacity\ ratio = \frac{actual\ hours\ available}{budgeted\ standard\ hours}$$

If the business has 10 production staff, all of whom work a 37.5 hour week, there are 375 standard hours available. If the budget requires 375 hours, then the capacity ratio = 1 or 100 per cent. No more work can be done unless the staff can complete the work in less than the standard time (is the standard time correct?) or they can work overtime. Otherwise you will have to recruit more staff or schedule the work for a different week (if possible).

Monitoring an overall schedule will help you to quote accurate delivery times and perhaps to spot gaps where you can fit in some extra work or devote more time, for example, to preparing the next promotional leaflet.

EXERCISE

Colin's Cabinets

Colin runs a business which manufactures steel filing cabinets. The manufacturing process includes cutting the sheet steel, folding, welding and riveting, assembling (runners, locks, etc.) and painting. From a formal time study and prior experience, Colin knows that the standard time to complete a cabinet shell is 25 minutes and for one drawer is 30 minutes. Painting requires 30 minutes. Final assembly and packing requires 5 minutes.

(a) What is the total standard time to complete a four-drawer filing cabinet?

(b) If your staff can actually complete a filing cabinet in 2 hours 30 minutes, what is the efficiency ratio?

(c) If you have five staff, who can carry out all the tasks equally well, how many hours' work might you have available in one year? (Think about how many hours a day and how many days a year each person might work.)

(d) If the actual number of hours available in a particular week is 130, say because of staff absence, what is the capacity ratio?

87

Conclusion and checklist

Many businesses run into difficulties, and some fail, because they do not price their work accurately. They fail to check the *actual* costs of a job against the *estimated* costs. While they cannot turn back history and reprice, they could at least amend their prices for future sales. Not doing this is likely to result in failing to achieve targets for profit and profitability.

Many businesses also, when preparing their annual accounts, look back over their work of the last year and wonder why they have achieved wildly different levels of profitability on different jobs. This is usually because they do not keep proper records (to which we will return in Chapter 8) or because they do not compare what they are doing with their own standards and targets. In this chapter, we have looked at:

- Defining different types of costs.
- Setting an hourly rate to recover overheads.
- Setting an item rate to recover overheads.
- Break-even analysis.
- Absorption costing.
- Marginal costing.
- Standard costing.

You need to decide the method that is most appropriate to your product or service and one that you are happy to use, then stick to it. You should continually review:

- The price at which you sell your product or service.
- Your costs – with the aim of reducing them.

Lastly, but perhaps most importantly, you need to be aware of your break-even point and of progress towards break even. As with other control figures, if you are not reaching the break even figure you will need to take corrective action

6

Planning capital assets

- Not only do you have to plan carefully for your trading activities you also have to plan carefully when you intend to acquire a major piece of equipment.
- The concept of depreciation will assist as a way of recovering the cost of capital assets over a number of years.
- You may need to decide between capital projects competing for available funds.
- You will need techniques for assessing the most cost effective means of acquisition – buy, lease or rent?

It is worth understanding how to compare costs of, and returns from, capital assets. Not only will this help in ensuring profitability, if you need to borrow the money it will assist in the preparation of financing proposals.

Planning fixed assets

Capital assets, or tangible fixed assets, are all those assets which require a capital investment – as opposed to current assets. They have a life of more than one year and generally require substantial expenditure. As with all other aspects of budgeting, you need to think carefully about whether you need a new piece of equipment or a freehold factory and how you are going to cover the cost.

Fixed assets are acquired for retention and use within the company. Money tied up in fixed assets, therefore, is not available for use as working capital. From that point of view, as little money as possible should be tied up in fixed assets. However, capital investments can be used to increase sales (by producing more) or reduce operating costs (by automation) so that a trade-off has to be made between the conflicting requirements of the business. The following points need to be considered before any investment is made:

- Will the investment produce a return consistent with the risk?

- Is there sufficient cash to pay for the investment? If additional capital has to be raised, is its cost justified?
- Has the investment been subjected to a rigorous evaluation?
  - consideration of other options;
  - technical justification;
  - consideration of implementation and timing; and
  - commercial viability.
- Have all the consequences of the investment been taken into consideration, for example, increased stock holding and additional staff requirements?

Equally, however, you do not want to allow all your machinery to become so old and dilapidated that it requires continual expense in repairs and leads to lost sales through being out of commission. New machines may give a better quality of finished product. It makes sense, therefore, to allow for some capital expenditure each year. This is best achieved with an integrated business plan and capital expenditure plan.

90

Optimum usage

Once fixed assets have been purchased they should be regularly reviewed to ensure that they are still contributing to the business.

The following points will need consideration:

- Each asset should be monitored to ensure it is still producing the required return on investment. This might be achieved by regularly calculating the ratio of sales (or production) to amount invested, or gross profit to amount invested.
- The expected future contribution from the asset may be below the disposal value in which case the asset should be sold. There may also be a case for replacing an asset with a newer, more efficient asset if the increased return on investment justifies the expenditure.
- Assets need to be properly maintained to ensure optimum profitability.
- Productivity may be improved by better production and planning methods.

Wear and tear

You will recall from Chapter 3 that depreciation is an annual allowance for wear and tear on equipment. Since tangible fixed assets have a life greater than one year it would clearly be unreasonable to attempt to recover the entire cost from your customers in the year of acquisition. Instead, the cost of the wearing out is spread over the expected life of the asset to ensure that this is passed on to your customers and to give you a satisfactory profit figure fairly. This fits with the matching principle also explained in Chapter 3.

Equipment, machinery and vehicles are depreciated, though generally land is not. Buildings are usually also depreciated, especially industrial buildings, though the increase in their value on the open market is often greater than the amount of depreciation. To calculate the annual depreciation, you need to estimate the expected life of the asset and be able to estimate any residual or scrap value, although this is often simply regarded as zero. There are two main methods for calculating depreciation – straight line and reducing balance.

Straight line depreciation

Straight line depreciation writes off a percentage of the purchase price each year. For example, a vehicle costing £12,000 and depreciated over four years could have 25 per cent of the purchase price (i.e. £3,000) charged to the profit and loss account each year.

EXAMPLE

Jumping Jane – Straight line depreciation

Jane has bought new equipment worth £30,000. She estimates that this will last seven years and have a scrap value of £2,000. The annual depreciation is, therefore, £4,000. This figure is included as one of the overhead costs in the profit and loss account. The 'book-value' (or written down value) of the fixed assets, as shown on the balance sheet, is reduced by this amount each year.

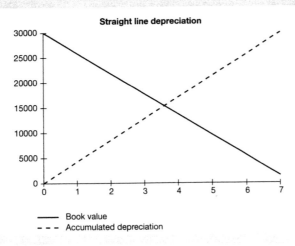

Straight line depreciation

——— Book value
– – – Accumulated depreciation

Reducing balance depreciation

Reducing balance depreciation is calculated as a percentage of the book value of the equipment. This gives the highest level depreciation in the first year, reducing as the equipment ages. This gives a truer reflection of the real value of the equipment, as anyone who has bought a new car knows! Additionally, as the equipment ages it might be expected that costs for repairs will increase each year. If the total cost of depreciation and repairs remains about constant, then arguably the price to charge your customers remains constant.

Jumping Jane – Reducing balance depreciation

Jane decides to use the reducing balance method, writing off her equipment over seven years. She charges 32 per cent depreciation annually.

Year	Depreciation	Balance
1	9,600	20,400
2	6,528	13,872
3	4,440	9,432
4	3,018	6,414
5	2,053	4,361
6	1,396	2,965
7	949	2,016

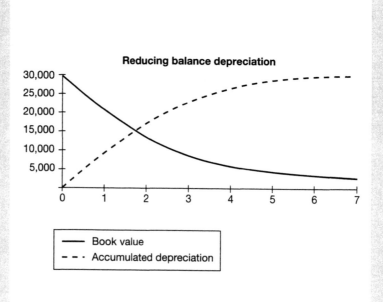

Reducing balance depreciation

— Book value
- - - Accumulated depreciation

If you know how many years (n) it will take fully to depreciate a piece of equipment, then you can calculate the rate, r, from this equation:

$$r = 100 - \left\{ \sqrt[n]{\frac{residual\ value}{original\ cost}} \times 100 \right\}$$

Depreciation in the accounts

Depreciation is simply a 'book transfer'. It does not involve any transfer of money, nor does it build up cash reserves to replace equipment in the future. It is, nevertheless, a cost to the business. It should, therefore, be included as an overhead cost in the profit and loss account. Depreciation is also normally shown in the balance sheet or sometimes as a note to explain how the value of fixed assets was derived. If possible, you should also aim to put aside a sum at least equal to the annual depreciation (preferably higher to allow for inflation) to ensure that you have the cash available when equipment does need to be replaced.

93

EXAMPLE

Katie's Kitchens – Fixed Assets

The example shows one way that depreciation is typically shown in accounts. Figures are shown for Katie's Kitchens since they are used in some of the exercises.

	Vehicles	Equipment	Premises	Total
Cost				
At 1 January 1994	14,000	16,000	50,000	80,000
Additions		3,216	36,784	40,000
Disposals				0
At 31 December 1994	14,000	19,216	86,784	120,000
Depreciation				
At 1 January 1994	8,000	10,000	6,000	24,000
Charge for year	3,500	5,765	1,736	11,000
At 31 December 1994	11,500	15,765	7,736	35,000
Net book value				
As at 31 December 1994	2,500	3,451	79,048	85,000
As at 31 December 1993	6,000	6,000	44,000	56,000

Tax considerations

Do not confuse depreciation with capital allowances for tax purposes. You may choose any level of depreciation that you think is appropriate. In the UK, when you submit your accounts to the Inland Revenue, they remove depreciation completely from their calculation of net profit. They then allow a capital allowance, generally, of 25 per cent on a reducing balance basis. For industrial buildings they allow 4 per cent per annum; there is no allowance for commercial buildings. If you expect your equipment and machines to last for at least four years, you may find it helpful to charge 25 per cent depreciation on a reducing balance basis each year also. Your profit calculation will then be similar to the Inland Revenue's calculation. If you expect equipment to last less than four years, such as computers, then write them off faster. Remember, the more accurately you reflect depreciation in your budget the more accurately you will be able to cost your product or service.

If you run a company, standard accounting practice sets down rules for depreciation of all fixed assets with limited useful lives.

Appraising capital investments

If capital investments are relatively small, it is unlikely that you will need special techniques to appraise them. But they are included here for two reasons. First, many suppliers now try to lease equipment to their customers rather than selling it directly. Do you know whether that is cheaper or more expensive than borrowing the money from the bank? Second, and more important, as businesses grow you may have opportunities to invest in new projects. Do you know how to appraise which one will give the best return?

> Decisions about major investments need to be made carefully, because often large sums of money will be involved and once a decision has been implemented it will be difficult to reverse.

As so often in business, the greatest difficulty will be in estimating the demand for the product, the likely trend and the price people will pay. You will also have to estimate the useful life of the assets, cost of maintenance, effect (positive or negative) on other aspects of your work, additional working capital required, etc.

When you make a capital investment, you do so because you expect to generate income in the future. If this were not the case, you would not make the investment. Thus, an investment appraisal compares cash outflows now with the likely cash inflows at some time in the future. Other key variables include the risk that your estimates are incorrect, likely tax allowance changes, inflation, etc. A comprehensive evaluation will attempt to allow for all of these.

There are a number of methods often used to appraise investment opportunities. The simplest, and least useful, is to compare total revenue with total expenditure. However, this ignores the cost of the money and ignores any time factor. Other methods include looking at the pay-back and discounted cash flows. The pay-back method looks at how long it takes for the business to recover its initial investment. You've probably done this yourself when considering installing double glazing or insulating the loft. How long will it take before the savings repay the initial investment? The most commonly used techniques, however, use discounted cash flow – either to calculate net present value or to calculate the internal rate of return.

EXAMPLE

Katie's Kitchens – Payback

Katie is considering spending £44,000 on new automated bench-forming equipment. She has looked carefully at the total costs involved and estimated the additional income that she is likely to generate as a direct result. She has then calculated the net profit for each quarter for the next three years.

She plots the cash flows on a bar chart, as shown in the dark shading in the figure. She has also plotted the cumulative position (in light shading) which shows that the machine will have paid for itself in three years.

95

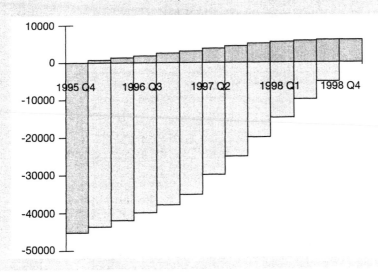

Return on capital

Some businesses look at the return on capital employed over the likely life of the asset or for a specific period.

In the example above the total outlay is £44,000. This is exactly paid back in three years so the average annual profit is £14,667. This represents an average return of 33 per cent. If the cost of borrowing the money, or the opportunity cost is less than 33 per cent then this is a project worth pursuing.

Discounting

Neither payback, nor appraisal looking at return on capital employed, allows for the cost of the money or the fact that a pound in your hand now is worth more than a pound in, say, one year's time. In larger business, the most common techniques use discounted cashflow: either to calculate net present value or to calculate the internal rate of return. £100 in your hand now is not the same as £100 receivable in, say, one year because money you have now could be earning interest. If the current rate of interest is 10 per cent, then the money you hold now will be worth £110 in one year. If this were reinvested, it would be worth £121 after a further year. This is known as compounding and can be formalised thus:

£100 now will be worth:
£100 x $(1 + r)$ in one year
£100 x $(1 + r)^2$ in two years
£100 x $(1 + r)^n$ in n years (where r is the current rate of interest expressed as a decimal)

So what is £100 receivable in n years worth now? It is the reverse of the above example. At an interest rate of 10 per cent:

£100 receivable in one year is worth $100/(1.1) = £91$ now
£100 receivable in two years is worth $100/(1.1)^2 = £83$ now

This procedure is the opposite of compounding and is called discounting. In other words, if you were given £83 now and invested it for two years at 10 per cent, it would by then be worth £100. Generally, we can say that:

£100 receivable in n years is worth $100/(1+r)^n$ (where r is the current rate of interest expressed as a decimal)

Discounted cash flow

A discounted cash flow (DCF) shows future cash flows, usually over several years, adjusted by a suitable rate, to take account of the timing of the cash flow. One method of comparing different options is to calculate the net present value (NPV) of each. An investment with a net present value which is positive is worth pursuing; if a choice has to be made, the investment with the highest NPV is the most profitable. The alternative is to calculate the internal rate of return (IRR). This is the estimated annual percentage profitability on the initial investment, once again allowing for the fact that future receipts are worth less than receipts today.

The IRR can be compared to the cost of the capital required or, in larger businesses, often to a predefined threshold. If it is higher than the cost of capital or the threshold, the investment is worth pursuing; the investment with the highest IRR is the most profitable. Remember however, that uncertainty also needs to be considered. The more risky a project, the higher IRR you will be seeking to compensate for the risk, but your assumptions may be less certain. You might, therefore, choose a lower level of risk and accept a lower IRR.

Net present value

97

The first step in calculating net present value is to estimate the cash flows, both positive and negative, for the expected life of the project (or, more often, the asset). The net cash flow is usually shown as the net profit, ignoring interest and tax. The capital expenditure is usually shown in period 0. These then need to be discounted to present values at a predetermined rate of interest. This is often taken as the cost of capital to your business, particularly appropriate if you will need to borrow the money from the bank. If you already have the money available, then use the opportunity cost, i.e. the rate of return you could achieve with the money on deposit.

If you have a computer or calculator, the discount factors can easily be calculated using the formula shown above, otherwise tables of discount factors are available to save you having to do the calculations.

EXAMPLE

Katie's Kitchens – Net present value

Katie has reconsidered the cost and returns on capital for the automated bench-forming equipment. She believes she can buy it at a cost of £40,000. She has estimated the net cash flows as shown below and used an interest rate of 10 per cent to calculate the discount factor, since she has the money in the bank and believes that 10 per cent is the best return she could get. Determining the cash flow may be difficult if overheads have to be spread over more than one machine. However, that is clearly essential if you are going to achieve an accurate answer.

Year	Cash flow	Discount factor	Present value
0	(40,000)	1.0000	(40,000)
1	3,000	.9091	2,727
2	11,000	.8264	9,091
3	14,000	.7513	10,518
4	16,000	.6830	10,928
5	18,000	.6209	11,177
NPV			4,441

The cash flows are multiplied by the discount factor to give the present values. These are totalled to give the net present value. In this case, the NPV is £4,441; this is positive so the return is greater than 10 per cent. In other words, the project is worth pursuing.

Suppose Katie has to borrow the money and has been offered a loan at an interest rate of 15 per cent. She now does the calculation again using different discount factors.

Year	Cash flow	Discount factor	Present value
0	(40,000)	1.0000	(40,000)
1	3,000	.8696	2,609
2	11,000	.7561	8,318
3	14,000	.6575	9,205
4	16,000	.5718	9,148
5	18,000	.4972	8,949
NPV			(1,771)

This time the NPV is negative. The project returns less than it costs to borrow the money so it is not worth doing purely in financial terms.

This technique can be used to compare the returns on different projects or on different ways of implementing the same project. Is it, for example, cheaper to borrow the money to buy outright or to lease the equipment?

Do not confuse the investment decision with the decision of whether to buy or lease. The decision whether to proceed with a project needs to be made first. Once you are certain that you wish to proceed, then you are ready to decide whether to buy or lease.

Buy or lease

You are wondering whether to buy or lease a new car. If you lease, you will have to make an immediate payment of £4,800 with two further payments in the following two years. In this example, the discount factors assume an opportunity cost of 14 per cent. This gives an NPV of £12,720. If you can buy the car for less money than this, buy it; otherwise, lease it (assuming the car becomes yours at the end of the three-year period. Otherwise include any additional purchase payments.) Remember that if you have to borrow the money, you must make the calculations with the interest rate which you will have to pay.

Year	Cash flow	Discount factor	Present value
0	4,800	1.0000	4,800
1	4,800	0.8772	4,224
2	4,800	0.7695	3,696
NPV			12,720

All these NPV calculations have assumed that interest rates stay constant for the period of the lease. A combination of inflation and a reducing interest rate may tip the scales in favour of leasing. So far, we have ignored the effects of tax and inflation on the DCF calculation. Unless you are good at seeing into the future, both are difficult to account for, but you may wish to adjust the cash flow figures in order to make some allowance for them. Inflation, particularly if it is high, will affect the real rate of return.

Imagine that your business has made a return of 15 per cent on capital and that the rate of inflation is 5 per cent – what is the real rate of return?

$$Real\ rate\ of\ return = \frac{1 + nominal\ rate\ of\ return}{1 + rate\ of\ inflation} - 1$$

Write the rates as decimals rather than as percentages: In our example, therefore, the real rate of return=1.15/1.05 −1=0.095 or nearly 10 per cent, as you might guess intuitively. While inflation is relatively low you don't need to worry about it too much. But if it starts to climb again, it will affect the rate of return which you will be seeking on your investment.

Internal rate of return

To calculate the internal rate of return, you will need to calculate a number of NPVs at different discount rates until an NPV of zero is achieved. This can be done quite easily on a computerised spreadsheet by choosing low and high interest rates. The discount rate when the NPV is equal to zero is the yield or return on investment for the project.

EXAMPLE

Katie's Kitchens – Internal rate of return

Choosing a rate of 13.46 per cent for Katie's Kitchens gives an NPV equal to zero:

Year	Cash flow	Discount factor	Present value
0	(40,000)	1.0000	(40,000)
1	3,000	.8814	2,644
2	11,000	.7768	8,545
3	14,000	.6847	9,585
4	16,000	.6034	9,654
5	18,000	.5318	9,573
NPV			0

100

If this yield is greater than the cost of borrowing the money, or greater than your predetermined yield, then undertake the project. Calculating the IRR is normally used by larger companies, who need to know the precise yield, and who have a minimum threshold below which they will not accept projects. If you ever decide to seek equity from a venture capital fund, they will use IRR calculations to help decide whether to invest. They normally have a pre-determined threshold which may be 35 per cent or higher.

It is also easy to determine the internal rate of return graphically as shown in the figure below. Pick two rates thought to be close to the likely rate of return. Calculate the NPV. Plot the results on a graph. Using the results from Katie's Kitchens gives a graph as shown. The actual rate of return can then be read from the graph as about 13.5 per cent which is close enough to the actual answer.

In an effort to keep the examples relatively simple, the impact of tax and the possible availability of grants has been ignored. These do however need to be included if you are assessing a proposal against a target return. If you are assessing competing investments, ensure both are treated in the same way.

Replacement of equipment

The examples so far have all been for taking decisions regarding the start of a new project or to assess the best method of paying for capital

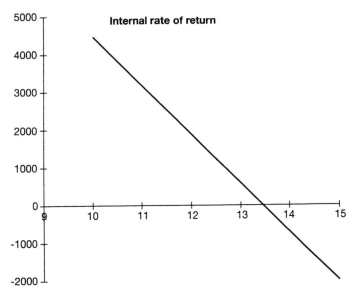

assets. Many buying decisions, however, have to be about whether to replace existing equipment. In some cases there may be little choice. The old equipment may be so worn out that it has to be replaced and the decision simply becomes one of how to pay. In other cases, the decision may not be so clear cut. New equipment may have a greater capacity or superior efficiency or provide a better quality. As with other purchasing decisions, you need to compare the options. What are the costs (running costs, repairs, depreciation, etc.) and what is the likely income (bearing in mind that greater capacity or better quality may, but not necessarily will, increase income) for each of the options?

Sometimes there are other issues which need to be considered – such as improved staff morale – when replacing old equipment. This is impossible to assess financially.

Funding capital assets

Equity, or shareholder capital, is the money introduced into a business by the proprietor(s) and anyone else willing to invest capital in the hope of getting future returns. If it is a company, then the equity is introduced in exchange for shares. If the business does well, the directors may declare a dividend each year. If it does very well, it may be floated on the Alternative Investments Market (AIM) or stock market, in which case the original shareholdings will become valuable. Often, though, shareholders' capital is locked into small businesses.

Loan capital, or debt, is money lent to a business. Normally, the period of the loan is determined according to the life of the asset for which it is used. A long-term loan for premises; a medium- or short-term loan for equipment; and an overdraft for working capital. Term loans are preferable to overdrafts since overdrafts are repayable on demand; however, it is unlikely that a term loan will be available for working capital. Interest on loans is tax deductible, whereas dividends are paid out of profit.

The purchase of buildings or land can probably be spread over 20 or 25 years with the asset used as security for the loan. It is unusual, however, for the banks to provide the entire sum required, preferring to limit their loan to 70 per cent of the value of the assets. Once you have built up a profitable track record with your bank, you should be able to attract medium-term loans, say three to seven years, to cover the cost of plant and equipment. The term of the loan will be dependent not only on the amount borrowed but also on the expected life of the equipment. Computers, for example, which rapidly become obsolete and increasingly expensive to repair, are unlikely to attract a loan of more than two or three years. Shop fittings, or office equipment, on the other hand, are likely to last a long time and need little maintenance, so you would be more easily able to obtain a loan over a longer period.

Sometimes long-term debt can be introduced as a debenture which normally receives a fixed rate of interest and is repayable in full at the end of the term. Debentures sometimes carry options to turn them into shares. Long-term debt is usually included with the capital on the balance sheet, whereas short-term debt, and especially overdrafts, are treated as current liabilities. Since most banks look for a gearing of around 50 per cent or less, once your business starts to grow, it will be essential to introduce more money as equity or else retain substantial profits in the business.

It is often possible for businesses to acquire equipment on hire purchase, lease or lease purchase. Lease companies will not usually have the same concerns about gearing as the banks. They will, however, be interested in the strength of your cash flow and whether you can afford the repayments.

With hire purchase the equipment becomes yours, though the finance provider may have certain rights over it until you have made all the payments. This has the advantage that you can claim the tax allowance.

With a leasing arrangement, the equipment will remain the property of the leasing company. The lessee has the legal right to use the equipment for the period of the lease assuming, of course, that the lease payments are up to date. At the end of the lease, the equipment reverts to the lessor, although it is often possible to buy the equipment for a small sum. With a lease purchase arrangement, the equipment automatically becomes the property of the purchaser on completion of all the payments.

EXERCISE

Eric's Engineering

Eric runs a mechanical engineering machine shop undertaking sub-contract work. He has £25,000 available to buy a new machine but cannot decide between a milling machine at £20,000 or a lathe at £25,000. He cannot afford both. He anticipates that the net cash flow for the next four years for the lathe will be £9,000 p.a .after which the lathe will be redundant. The milling machine will only generate £7,000 net p.a. but it will last for six years. He could achieve 10 per cent long term if he simply invested the money. Does he buy a machine and, if so, which one?

103

Assessing risk

Before you finally go ahead with any major purchase it makes sense to undertake an overall assessment of the likely risk. As part of the planning process you will have already considered all the costs and all the income associated with the initiative. Usually these will have been prepared as cash flow forecasts so it will help to prepare profit and loss and balance sheet forecasts also.

- Consider the break-even point?
- Think about the sensitivity to changes in the forecasts. What happens if costs rise or sales fall? What effect will that have on profitability. Sensitivity analysis will be explained in more detail in the next chapter.
- If you are borrowing the money what is the effect on your gearing and interest cover? Will the bank still be happy?

Conclusion and checklist

Too often, little thought is given to planning the acquisition of capital assets. Even when acquisition is essential, little thought is given to how the equipment should be paid for; whether outright purchase is best, even with the cost of borrowing the money, or whether a lease or rental arrangement may be more cost effective.

There are a number of ways of assessing whether you should invest in a particular project. The objective of every technique is to help you decide whether the return on capital you will make is sufficient to make the project attractive. For larger businesses, this becomes a very simple exercise which simply compares the returns available from different opportunities. For smaller businesses, inevitably there are intangible returns also. For example, failure to invest may threaten the future of the business. Jobs, particularly of the principals, may be at stake. Logically, if business proprietors cannot get a sufficient return, then they should work for someone else and invest their money in a different way. Practically, they may not be able to get a job elsewhere, or may not want to, and so this needs to be taken into account. Nevertheless, the appraisal techniques shown can still be used to choose between options to calculate the returns likely to be achieved. The information can then be used as part of a broader decision-making process.

Lastly, the results of your capital planning will need to be incorporated into the overall plan for the business. This is the subject of the next chapter. Actual performance will need to be compared with the forecast.

Formulating the plan

In Chapter 2 it was explained that the budget is simply the operating plan set out in financial terms. In order to retain control of your business.

- **You need to have a plan and objectives against which you can measure your performance.**
- **This requires you to understand the process of budgeting and preparing a financial plan.**
- **You will also need to consider the sensitivity of the budgets to changes in the market place.**

The starting point

The starting point in preparing any plan has to be the setting of targets. Of course, your market research may give a feel for the likely level of sales for, say, the next couple of years. If that forecast shows sales which are too low, then you will have to do something about it: change product, improve your marketing or give up your business and work for someone else.

In Chapter 4 the concept of ratio analysis was introduced as a way of interpreting accounts. Ratios can also assist you in controlling your business by using them to set financial targets. Ideally, you should only have a small number of targets, as that makes it easier to exercise control. Furthermore, as all the ratios are linked, keeping control of a few will ensure that you keep control of all of them. You may find it helpful to look again at the ratio tree on page 61.

The first target should be one that defines return on capital. If a large proportion of the capital employed is equity, I suggest that you use return on equity (RoE) though it doesn't really matter which definition of capital you use. If you only have a low proportion of equity compared to borrowed funds (that is, you have a high gearing) then I suggest that you use return on capital employed (RoCE) instead. If it's your money, the return needs to be higher than the return you could get elsewhere; if you are mostly using borrowed money, then the return needs at least to be higher than the cost of borrowing the money.

Once you've determined a figure for return on capital, you can define the net profit required, both as a percentage and in absolute terms. If you are self-employed, remember that your drawings are part of the profit so either you need a profit margin high enough to allow for drawings, or else you need to include your drawings as part of the fixed costs. Provided you have a feel for the likely costs, you can now set targets for gross profit and gross profit margin. This will define the minimum level of sales required by value.

Does this level of sales seem realistic? How does it compare with last year's sales? Look at the total market – is it expanding or contracting? Talk to your customers about their likely use of your product or service next year. What marketing are you planning to attract new customers? If you employ sales people, ensure they bring back market intelligence. If you are already in business, you will almost certainly have some historical data on which you can base your estimate.

You need to estimate your sales both by value and volume. Are you aware of the effect of price on your product? Have you monitored how demand changes with price changes? If not, this is data that you should be aiming to collect in future. You will probably have a record of the sale price for successful sales, but also record the sale price for unsuccessful sales. If possible, discover what prices are being charged by your competitors. Sometimes this is easy; in retail, for example. Sometimes it is more difficult.

> If you lose a contract, telephone and find out why. Did you lose on price? Did you lose on quality? Did you lose because your delivery date was too slow? This is all useful market intelligence and will help you to build and to maintain an overview of the market.

When you win a contract, you should also try to find out why your customers preferred you. Do not take your customers for granted.

It is also helpful to know the effects of other activities on sales. What is the effect of advertising expenditure, for example? This is often difficult to monitor, especially if you advertise regularly and/or in several different ways. Advertising tends to have a cumulative effect; a series of advertisements is likely to generate more sales than one occasional advert. Nevertheless, you should attempt to discover how customers find out about you. Record increases in sales, if any, when you advertise. Only change one advertising variable at a time. If you do this carefully over several months, you should be able to build up an overall picture of the effect of advertising. This, too, can be plotted on a graph for ease of understanding. Sales may increase simply through the cumulative effect of advertising over a number of years, word of mouth, etc. Plot sales over time – it is then possible to calculate trends by means of moving averages or regression analysis.

If you have just started up, or are introducing a new product, then these techniques will be of little help. On the other hand, you should have some detailed market research to call upon. Watch your competitors. Request copies of their annual reports; these are all filed annually at Companies House and are available for a small fee. Look at Extel and McCarthy information at your library. Most libraries have, or can obtain, copies of market research reports from Mintel, Key Notes, etc. Some industries and trade associations publish market intelligence. Glenigan, for example, publishes a monthly summary of all major building contracts to help businesses in the construction industry. Most important of all, talk to your prospective customers.

The forecast will also need to take account of current orders and enquiries, competitors' price and market share, proposed marketing strategy, general economic outlook, etc. Then set a sales target for the year and, ideally, break it down by month either as a cumulative target as shown below or as a bar chart showing sales targets for each month individually.

107

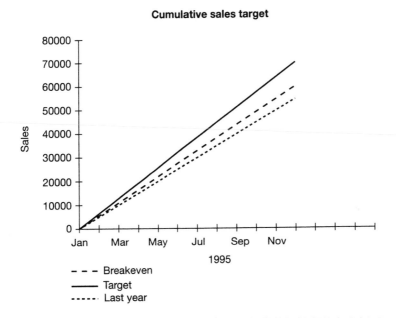

Cumulative sales target

The forecasting and budgeting process is very important; you are committing yourself to work to that level of sales. Without the contribution those sales generate, you will be unable to cover all your overhead costs.

You may need to break down your sales forecast by grographic area and allow for seasonal variation. Once you have prepared your forecast, you are ready to set out your sales budget. The budgeting process is normally carried out just once each year.

The sales budget

The sales budget should set out the number of units that you might be able to sell at a given price broken down by product, area, timing, etc. The sales budget is required to provide overall targets; you will need it to prepare the other budgets.

Volume: Product A

	UK	Europe	USA	Total
Qtr 1	1,000	350	150	1,500
Qtr 2	1,000	350	150	1,500
Qtr 3	1,000	350	150	1,500
Qtr 4	1,000	350	150	1,500
Total	4,000	1,400	600	6,000

A budget by volume is shown above. Normally, sales should be shown on a monthly basis for the year, although in this case the sales budget has been summarised into quarters. The table below shows the budget transferred into values, assuming a price of £51 per unit.

Value: Product A

	UK	Europe	USA	Total
Qtr 1	51,000	17,850	7,650	76,500
Qtr 2	51,000	17,850	7,650	76,500
Qtr 3	51,000	17,850	7,650	76,500
Qtr 4	51,000	17,850	7,650	76,500
Total	204,000	71,400	30,600	306,000

Production budgets

Once the sales budget has been determined, you are able to prepare a production budget. This budgets for the costs which vary with the level of production. These are mostly just the direct costs. At Katie's Kitchens, the only direct costs are the raw material costs. Don't forget to include sub-contract and direct labour costs if appropriate to your business. The materials usage budget, sub-contract budget and direct labour budgets should reflect the sales budget, including any discounts that you anticipate may be necessary to achieve that level of sales. For larger businesses, it may be helpful to forecast labour requirements by type of labour. This will assist in identifying surplus or shortfalls. If you use sales people working on commission, their commission is usually shown as a direct cost (though their retainer, if they have one, would be a fixed cost). Discounts are usually shown in the budget as a direct cost (even though in reality a discount is simply income foregone).

If there are other variable costs, such as electric power consumption, these should also be assessed to give a total production budget.

Materials usage budget: Product A		
	Units	£
Qtr 1	1,500	37,200
Qtr 2	1,500	37,200
Qtr 3	1,500	37,200
Qtr 4	1,500	37,200
Total	6,000	148,800

The materials purchase budget

If you have a manufacturing business, the next step after the sales budget is to look at the raw materials holding and ordering requirements. An example is shown below:

If there are likely to be delays receiving raw materials after ordering

Materials purchase budget			
	Ordered	Consumed	Balance
Opening balance			8,000
Qtr 1	40,000	37,200	10,800
Qtr 2	40,000	37,200	13,600
Qtr 3	40,000	37,200	16,400
Qtr 4	40,000	37,200	19,200
Total	160,000	148,800	19,200

them you will need to hold sufficient raw materials to cover production for the typical period of delay. This ties up working capital so your target should be to keep raw materials to a minimum.

Purchasing policy should be reviewed regularly to ensure that you are obtaining value for money from suppliers and that you are paying the lowest possible price consistent with the quality desired.

You may be able to identify possible discounts or rebates which can also be built into the materials budget. Once raw materials have been issued to production they become *work in progress*. Work in progress, valued at least at the cost of the raw materials that are now in production is often shown on the balance sheet, though arguably it has no value until there is a product capable of being sold. If the manufacturing process is a long one, then the value added at each stage (labour, resources, etc.) also has to be financed until the product is sold so this increases the working capital requirement.

When preparing the production budget, remember to watch for the number of machine hours available, the number of labour hours available, etc. If you exceed your capacity you may have problems. On the other hand, you do not want expensive machinery lying idle. So you should also look at your utilisation rates – if they are too low, can you increase them, perhaps by increasing sales or introducing new products?

Stock control

If you do not carry much stock, you may wish to skip this section. If, however, you have large amounts of working capital tied up in stock, then you need to plan and monitor your stock position carefully, as raw materials are bought and consumed, as work in progress continues through the factory and as finished goods are sold. Some businesses, such as retailers, buy in finished goods, but they still need effective stock control.

Economic order quantities

Do you wait until you have run out of raw materials before you re-order? Do you know the optimum amount to order at one time? Do you minimise working capital tied up in stock?

Simple stock control systems are usually designed so that when stock falls to a predetermined level, then you re-order. That level should provide sufficient stock to cover the expected delay between placing the order and receiving the goods, plus allowance for a contingency. Here is an example of a very simple stock ordering reminder system. This can act as a back-up to your stock record book. Most computerised book-keeping systems can include a stock control module if desired.

EXAMPLE

Ian's Inducements

Ian runs a business offering direct mail facilities to other businesses. As a result, he has to hold large stocks of envelopes. He knows from experience how many boxes of each size of envelope to hold as a minimum stock requirement. He stacks his boxes in columns. On top of the minimum stock holding for each size, Ian places a red card. Further boxes are then stacked on top. When the envelopes are used down to the red card, Ian knows that it is time to re-order.

As explained earlier, you do not want to tie up too much working capital in stock. Costs of holding stock include rent on the space occupied, insurance, interest foregone on the money, etc. On the other hand, running out of raw materials can be extremely embarrassing. You may have to pay extra for rapid delivery of new stock. Production will be halted and you will lose sales. The process of ordering needs time and therefore costs money also. These costs can be shown graphically. Adding the costs together gives a total cost curve. As can be seen there is an optimum order volume, Q at the trough in the total cost curve.

Economic order quantity

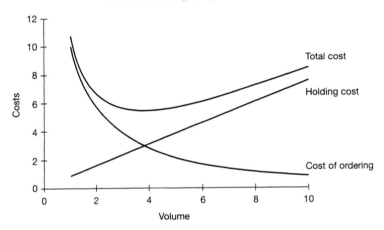

111

The economic order quantity, Q is given by the equation:

$$Q = \sqrt{\frac{2UO}{H}}$$

where U is the usage during a defined period, O is the cost of ordering (administration, handling, quality assessment), and H is the holding cost of one item.

EXAMPLE

Sally's Slates

Sally has a roofing business and has to ensure that she always has enough slates in stock. She has found from experience that she needs around 100,000 slates in one year. These cost £2 each. She estimates that the total cost of placing an order is about £50 and that the warehousing cost of each slate is about 25p. Thus

$$Q = \sqrt{\frac{2 \times 1000,000 \times 50}{0.25}} = 6,325$$

So the economic order quantity is 6325 per order. If Sally orders that number each time, she will have to order 16 times per year.

If demand, and therefore your usage, fluctuates, or if the price changes frequently, or if there are long lead times, there will be no benefit from using this analysis. On the other hand, for many businesses, it can lead to a reduction in stock holding costs and improved efficiency.

Just-in-time stock control

Just-in-time stock control has been around for a long time though it is primarily the Japanese who have developed it. The objective is that deliveries of raw materials or bought-in components should arrive just in time to be included in the process. This saves holding large amounts of stock tying up working capital and space. It is often difficult to organise without the muscle that Nissan or Toyota commands. It requires extremely good planning and can easily cause problems if delivery is 'just too late'.

EXAMPLE

Henry's Headboards

Do not think you have to be large to use a just-in-time delivery system. Henry runs a business which manufactures headboards for beds. He sells on customer service guaranteeing delivery within the week for orders placed at the beginning of the week. Because his premises are not very large and because he cannot afford to tie up working capital in large stock holdings, he orders wood and upholstery every Thursday for delivery on the following Monday. Foam presents a fire risk so he is limited in the total amount he can store at his premises. As a result, he has foam delivered three times per week.

Once you get into the habit, just-in-time stock control is just as easy as any other system. A major advantage of just-in-time stock control is that the need to value raw material stock and finished goods stock is reduced substantially since stock no longer requires large amounts of working capital.

Material Resource Planning

Material Resource Planning (MRP) is a sophisticated computer based planning and control system used by businesses manufacturing an end product made from a large number of parts and sub-assemblies. The aim is to ensure that the right number of parts all come together at the right time throughout the production process. This allows businesses to limit the level of stock and work in progress but also ensure that there is always sufficient to avoid disruption at all stages of production.

Shrinkage

Many businesses suffer from shrinkage (theft) and shop-lifting. Ideally your stock control system will indicate at an early stage if this is happening. You may need to take regular stock checks. Does the amount of actual stock reconcile with your stock control book? It is often difficult to prevent this completely. Take some simple precautions. Keep stock locked away. Ensure stock is deducted correctly in the control book and signed for. Be very vigilant.

The overheads budget

Once the production budget has been prepared, the other costs need to be calculated. If you are in manufacturing, it is likely that these will represent a relatively small proportion of the total costs. On the other hand, if you are running a service sector business, it is likely that the overheads will represent a very high proportion or, indeed, all of the cost. If you have decided to use ratios which assess costs as a proportion of sales, then it makes sense to build up your overheads budget using the same cost groupings. Don't forget to include overhead costs which appear 'below the line' such as interest or drawings.

113

In the example, the overheads budget is shown for the business, not by product. You may, if you choose, aim to allocate the overheads to each product or you may prefer to retain overheads as a single budget. You will, however, have to ensure that the price for each product makes a reasonable contribution to the overheads.

Overheads budget		
Production		
Salaries	205,000	
Premises	11,000	
		216,000
Administration		
Salaries	35,000	
Insurance	2,000	
Other	2,000	
		39,000
Marketing		33,000
Distribution		36,000
Interest		25,000
		349,000

The production cost budget

You are now in a position to pull together the production budget and the overheads budget into a single production cost budget. If you have more than one product, then you will have a production budget for each product. You will also have variable overheads to add for each product. There is no need to split fixed overheads across products at this point since you are trying to determine the total costs. On the other hand, if some of the costs have been collected on a product or a departmental basis, then it probably makes sense to keep them separate, even at this stage, provided they are all included.

The capital expenditure budget

If you expect to spend large sums on capital equipment, then you need to set a budget and determine likely timing for those purchases. This is essential information if you are to prepare an accurate forecast. If you do not have all of the cash available to buy equipment then you will need to negotiate a loan. You will need to include the cost of borrowing (i.e. interest) and depreciation in your overheads budget. You will need to know the repayment schedule for your cash flow forecast.

If you decide to lease equipment, make sure that you read all the small print. While the selling is carried out by your supplier, the leasing is done by a finance company. Usually the conditions are more favourable for them than for you. On the other hand, the lessor usually has a responsibility to ensure the equipment keeps working even if the supplier can no longer support you.

Preparing financial forecasts

You now have nearly all the information required to prepare your financial forecast. A cash flow forecast sets out, usually on a month by month basis for the following 12 months, all receipts and all payments from the business. Remember that it only shows cash in and out, so non-cash items such as depreciation are ignored.

Before you can complete the forecast you need to estimate the length of time it will take to collect money from your customers and the length of time before you expect to settle with your suppliers. In western Europe, businesses can normally expect to wait at least 30 days and more usually 60 days from issuing an invoice until they are paid but some industries typically take far longer. Some businesses, however, successfully ask for deposits or staged payments. This helps their cash flow. Businesses should aim for their settlement target to be no shorter than their collection period but they may find some suppliers impose strict terms of settlement in say 30 days. Businesses should take this into account when preparing their cash flow forecast.

You should now be in a position to set out all the information in a month by month summary of the cash inflows and outflows for your business. The cash flow forecast should include receipts of cash from customers; payments for raw materials; payments of all other expenses; staff wages and, separately, your drawings; capital expenditure; grants or loans and loan repayments; VAT receipts and VAT repayments; corporation tax; etc. All of these items should normally be shown separately and should be shown in the month in which the money will be paid into your business or will be paid out by it. For businesses with a modest turnover, and which demonstrate profitability in the year, it is normal only to forecast one year ahead, with a monthly cash flow.

Larger businesses, especially those seeking equity investments and/or which do not show profitability in the year may need to prepare forecasts for two or three years. The first year cash flow is usually shown monthly, the second year quarterly and the third year just a single figure. It also helps in assessing the business, and therefore assists prospective funders, if you can include forecasts of P & L and balance sheet, otherwise the appraiser will have to construct them from the information provided. In summary, the cashflow forecast should include:

- Receipts of cash from customers.
- Payments for raw materials.
- Payments for all other expenses.
- Drawings and wages.
- Capital expenditure.
- Capital, loans or grants introduced.
- Loan repayments.
- VAT receipts and payments (if VAT registered).
- Tax payments.

It is normal to show all of these items separately. They must be shown in the month in which they will occur, as shown in the example below.

EXAMPLE

Catherine's Chairs – Cash flow

Let us look at the cash flow for Catherine's Chairs which only shows four months' figures. Catherine makes high quality wooden chairs. She starts off the period with some stock on hand and for which she will pay in July (and for which VAT is recoverable from Customs & Excise in July). She aims to purchase sufficient raw materials each month to cover her production for the month plus a little extra in order to build up a buffer in case of delivery delays. She pays for raw materials in the month following delivery. Her stock movements are as shown below.

Stock movements

	July	*August*	*Sept*	*Oct*	*Total*
Opening stock	1,000	800	1,600	1,800	1,000
Purchases	4,000	5,000	5,000	5,000	19,000
Usage	4,200	4,200	4,800	5,400	18,600
Closing stock	800	1,600	1,800	1,400	1,400

She expects to sell the bulk of what she makes and to be paid one third of the total sales immediately, one third in the month following the sale and the last third in the next month.

Cash flow statement

	July	*August*	*Sept*	*Oct*	*Total*	*Accruals*
Sales by value	8,400	8,400	9,600	10,800	37,200	
Receipts						
Cash	2,800	2,800	3,200	3,600	12,400	
Debtors		2,800	5,600	6,000	14,400	10,400
VAT	490	980	1,540	1,680	4,690	1,820
Loans	5,000				5,000	
Total	8,290	6,580	10,340	11,280	36,490	12,220
Payments						
Trade creditors	1,000	4,000	5,000	5,000	15,000	5,000
Overheads	1,600	1,600	1,600	1,600	6,400	
Equipment					0	
Wages	1,000	1,000	1,000	1,000	4,000	
Loan repayments	400	400	400	400	1,600	
Interest	50	50	50	50	200	
Drawings	1,000	1,000	1,000	1,000	4,000	
VAT	455	980	1,155	1,155	3,745	875
VAT to C&E	(175)			1,330	1,155	735
Total	5,330	9,030	10,205	11,535	36,100	
Monthly balance	2,960	(2,450)	135	(255)	390	
Opening balance	0	2,960	510	645		
Closing balance	2,960	510	645	390		

Note that this cash flow forecast has an extra row to show sales by value. Strictly speaking, that is not part of the cashflow. The cash for these sales is shown in the month it is received. There is also an extra column to show any cash still owing to or owed by the business at the end of the period. This will help in the preparation of profit and loss accounts and balance sheets.

As can be seen, Catherine requires working capital of around £5,000, that is, the level of the loan shown in the first month. Working capital might come from the owners or from the business's own resources or the business might need to borrow it from the bank.

It is often helpful when preparing cash flow forecasts initially to ignore any finance that is available from the principals or from a bank. The cash flow forecast then shows the true position of the business and can be used constructively to decide if the budget is viable and can be adjusted to reflect the true position.

When preparing budgets, remember to allow for increased costs, for instance, due to inflation or future pay awards. You should also allow contingency sums – for example, for repairs to machinery. If you do need a loan, then you will also need to allow an amount for loan interest. If you use equipment, remember to allow for depreciation. While depreciation is not included in the cash budget, you may need to allow for the replacement or repairs of machinery.

117

If you have a term loan, the capital repayments will not figure in your profit and loss account – they are not a business expense – although the interest portion of the repayments will be charged as an expense. However, the repayments do need to be included in your cash flow forecast.

EXERCISE

Financial forecasting

Prepare a cash flow forecast for your business for the next 12 months. What is the maximum expected deficit? Are there likely to be higher deficits during any month?

Now prepare a profit and loss account and a balance sheet based on your cash flow forecast. Does your balance sheet balance?

Working Capital Requirements

As explained in the working capital cycle in Chapter 1, you need to have enough working capital to cover the payments that you have to make while you wait for receipts from your customers. There are, effectively, four sources of money for working capital. It might come from money introduced by the owner(s). It might come from retained earnings as the business makes a profit. It might be 'borrowed' from your suppliers by making them wait longer than the time taken by your customers to pay you. If these sources do not provide sufficient working capital then you will have to borrow it from the banks, usually as an overdraft. If you have got your forecasts right, then you should have a fair idea of what the income and expenditure is likely to be and, therefore, the level of overdraft required, if any.

Since the amount of working capital required changes frequently, it makes sense to utilise an overdraft to cover this requirement. The disadvantage of an overdraft is that it is repayable on demand. Term loans, on the other hand, are repayable over the term of the loan and cannot generally be recalled early. The size of overdraft required clearly depends on the working capital requirement and has to be agreed at least annually with your bank manager.

The cash flow forecast provides an estimate of the likely requirement. However, this is prone to error. Receipts may be delayed by two or three weeks, pushing up the requirement in the middle of a month, though this may not be reflected in month end figures.

118

EXAMPLE

Gary's Graphics

Gary runs a graphic design business. His business starts in January with average invoiced sales of £5,000 per month, but expects to wait an average of 60 days for payment. In other words, sales of £5,000 in January only produces receipts in March. He has no credit terms from his suppliers, paying for everything immediately. His cash flow forecast is as shown:

Cash flow statement

	January	February	March
Receipts			5,000
Expenses			
Materials	1,000	1,000	1,000
Overheads	2,500	2,500	2,500
Drawings	1,000	1,000	1,000
	4,500	4,500	4,500
Balance	(4,500)	(4,500)	500
Cumulative balance	(4,500)	(9,000)	(8,500)

It appears from the cash flow forecast, therefore, that Gary has a peak requirement of £9,000.

Customers will generally delay payments to you for as long as possible, though you cannot always do this to your suppliers, especially if you are a small business. As a rule of thumb, it makes sense to aim for minimum working capital of a month's average sales multiplied by the number of months before you expect to be paid. If you hold large levels of stock and want to be rather more accurate, then use the following procedure:

	Months
Determine average number of weeks raw material is held in stock: e.g.	1.5
Deduct: credit period from suppliers	(1)
Add: average number of weeks to produce goods or service	0.5
Add: average number of weeks finished goods are in stock	0.5
Add: average time customers take to pay	2
Total	3.5

The working capital requirement is then the average monthly sales multiplied by the number of months. If sales are growing strongly, the working capital requirement will increase commensurately. In this case, it might be helpful to use peak monthly sales multiplied by the number of months proportionately. If sales for the year are estimated at £500,000 then the maximum working capital required is (3.5/12) x 500,000=£146,000. It would be more accurate, however, to use the cost of sales (direct and fixed) rather than the full selling price.

119

If the business is growing, then the working capital requirement will grow also. You need to watch for this, since it may mean that a larger overdraft is required.

Factoring and invoice discounting

You might choose to speed up payments for your supplies by factoring or invoice discounting. There are a number of factoring agents who will take your invoices and give you a proportion of the total, around 80–90 per cent, immediately. The balance is paid when the customer pays the factor, less their commission which is often around 3–4 per cent. A non-recourse factor will also provide protection against bad debts, though there will be an additional charge for this of around 1–3 per cent. Factoring is therefore an expensive way of speeding up cash flow. Depending on your specific factoring agreement, it may take away all the effort of chasing up the slow payers. For some businesses the cost often equates to a full-time person who might otherwise be employed to monitor the sales ledger and chase the debtors, so it is worth doing. Factoring is not normally available until you have been in business for three years and your turnover is at least £250,000 p.a. You should read the small print carefully: some factors recharge you for invoices not settled within an agreed period which will give back to you all the cash flow problems that factoring is intended to remove; they may refuse to accept invoices to customers with a poor credit rating.

With invoice discounting, you sell on to a discounter the face value of your invoices less their commission. You still retain control of your sales ledger, however, and you are still responsible for chasing slow payments – it is beneficial in that your customers still send their payments to you direct and it is not therefore apparent to them that you discount the invoices.

If you use either factoring or invoice discounting, review the cost regularly. Compare it with the cost of having an overdraft. Would it cost you less? Can you sell the time you save at a price greater than the cost of the factor? Of course, it may be that you cannot persuade a bank to lend you the money so you may have little choice. In general, however, at least for small businesses factoring is an expensive way of borrowing money and once you have entered a factoring arrangement, it can be difficult to get out of it.

120

Sensitivity analysis

It is important to know how sensitive your forecast is to changes. Sensitivity analysis looks at 'what if …' questions. What happens to your cash position, for example, if sales fall by 10 per cent? What happens if your main supplier increases raw material prices by 12 per cent? Sensitivity analysis is particularly used by financial institutions when considering propositions for a loan. If your business is particularly susceptible to small changes, then you probably do not have a sufficiently large profit margin. You will thus be less likely to receive the loan required. Of course, you may not be able simply to increase prices to improve your margins – that might deter customers. You may find it difficult to cut costs. Are there other ways, however, in which you can push up the margins – increasing output, for example?

Catherine's Chairs – Sensitivity analysis

	July	August	Sept	Oct	Total
Sales by value	8,400	8,400	9,600	10,800	37,200
Receipts	8,290	6,580	10,340	11,280	36,490
Costs	5,330	9,030	10,205	11,535	36,100
Balance	2,960	(2,450)	135	(255)	390
Sales down by 10%	7,560	7,560	8,640	9,720	33,480
Receipts	7,461	5,922	9,306	10,152	32,841
Costs	5,213	8,560	9,618	10,948	34,338
Balance	2,249	(2,638)	(312)	(796)	(1,497)
Cumulative balance	2,249	(389)	(701)	(1,497)	

Look at the figures. A drop of sales of 10 per cent leads to an increase in the loan or overdraft required, (from £5,000 to £6,500) but a substantial drop in overall profitability from making a small profit to now making a loss.

121

Having undertaken your sensitivity analysis, you may need to review elements of your budget. Sensitivity analysis can help in making decisions. You may want to consider, for example, the effect of increased raw material, labour or overhead costs; of reducing prices, with constant volumes, to counteract competitors; or reducing volumes, with constant prices, due to over-optimistic forecasts. Furthermore, if you are about to spend a large sum of money on equipment, you may want to look ahead several years if at all possible.

Sensitivity analysis

Go back to the cash flow forecast that you prepared in the last exercise.
(a) What is your overdraft requirement?
(b) What happens if your sales are 20 per cent lower than forecast?
(c) What happens if your raw material costs rise by 15 per cent?

Conclusion and checklist

Formulating your plan consists of:

- Identifying your strategic objectives;
- Defining operational objectives;
- Preparing and agreeing a master budget; and
- Ensuring that everyone with a responsibility for achieving objectives, financial or otherwise, is aware of, and has agreed with, those objectives.

A business plan, of course, will require an analysis of the market and a marketing strategy. This chapter has only been concerned with the financial aspects of the business plan. It needs to include:

- A sales forecast and sales budget.
- A production budget.
- A materials purchase budget.
- A labour budget.
- An overheads budget.
- A production cost budget.
- A cash budget.

Preparing the sales forecast is the hardest part of producing any plan, especially for a new business. Monitor what happens to sales when you change price. Collect market intelligence by watching your competitors and quizzing your customers. If a systematic approach is used, the interactions between the various elements will become apparent. Pitfalls will be anticipated which might not otherwise come to light. Remember, you may not get your plan absolutely right first time – you may need several attempts, improving each time, before you produce a workable document. You need to ensure in the completed budget that:

- All parts are consistent with one another.
- It represents an achievable plan which maximises profit.
- The budgeted profit is adequate to ensure the business's survival and growth.
- All costs are contained and controlled.
- Accounting records are adequate.
- There will be no cash flow problems.

It is important that you drive the budgeting and planning process. There are businesses where budgets have been tried and subsequently failed. This usually happens because the process has not been implemented correctly. Some common pitfalls include:

- Budgets cannot work without an effective business structure. Budgets are not a substitute for organisation.
- Budgets will not solve the problems of poor management.
- Imposed budgets cause frustration and resentment – they are doomed to failure in the long term.
- Care should be taken to ensure that budgets do not become cumbersome, meaningless or expensive.
- The plans should not become too inflexible. The real world changes from day to day.
- Sometimes events overtake the plan and a new plan becomes necessary.

Part 4

.

Exercising Control

8

Collecting the information

> ■ It is essential to keep appropriate financial records in a simple and straightforward manner to provide management accounts and to satisfy external obligations.
> ■ A carefully planned book-keeping system, possibly computerised, will help you to do this effectively and in such a way that control figures can be easily derived.

This chapter is primarily intended to introduce the principles of book-keeping – both single entry and double entry – and to explain the advantages of using a computer based accounting system. If you already understand the principles, or are not involved in book-keeping, you may wish to skip this chapter.

In the first chapter, the importance of planning and then monitoring performance against the plan was emphasised. Chapter 9 will suggest ways of analysing the data to give feedback about performance. This is only possible if the right data is collected and recorded. A great deal of data can be recorded about your business and it is particularly easy with computers to get carried away and record too much. It is important to identify what is likely to be helpful for your particular circumstances, and then to use the information derived to provide effective control.

A business must record every financial transaction. How it does this will depend on the size and nature of the business and on the staff resource available. A business run entirely on cash will need only a cash book plus the supporting invoices. However, very few businesses are entirely run on cash in this age of credit. Like cash, credit needs to be carefully controlled to ensure the health of the business. If all these records are kept well and are easy to read, not only will they provide the information that you need, but they will also make it easier for you or your accountant to prepare your end of year accounts. The end of year accounts are fine for the shareholders and the Inland Revenue, but they are produced far too late to exercise tight control. For that, you require management accounts, produced regularly and giving the essential information to help you and your staff ensure that you are on target.

Accounting records are not only the books used to record the business transactions but also include all the invoices both issued and received by the business. The business should file its records in an orderly manner, including purchase invoices and copy sales invoices, as this will assist in keeping accurate accounting records.

What records should you keep?

All your financial information is derived from your book-keeping system. While some of the techniques may appear more appropriate for larger businesses, they will all help very small businesses as well. A reliable, easy to use accounting system is, therefore, essential if your monitoring is going to be straightforward and if your control is to be effective. It is easy to underestimate the problems encountered in collecting relevant data, so take the time and thought to set up an effective and efficient system.

In the early stages of running a business, the most cost-effective method of book-keeping is to keep the books manually. A good book-keeping system will provide you with all the information needed regularly to compare your business's performance with your plan. In due course, you may computerise or buy in a book-keeper, but it will still be helpful to understand how the book-keeping works. There are many computerised book-keeping systems available but it probably makes sense first to set up a manual system which you completely understand. The danger of not understanding the system is that errors, which inevitably creep in, will not be spotted.

126

Whether you use a proprietary book-keeping system or set up your own using cash analysis books, you need a system which will enable you to collect all the relevant data and convert that data to provide you with up-to-date, accurate and meaningful management accounts.

The data to record include:

- Sales orders received.
- Invoices issued by the business for sales.
- Purchase orders placed by the business.
- Invoices received by the business for purchases.
- Cash receipts.
- Cash expenditure.

This data will enable you to prepare:

- Production schedules.
- Purchasing requirements.
- Management accounts (including regular bank reconciliations).

and to monitor:

- Profitability and efficiency.
- Liquidity and solvency.
- Stock levels of raw materials, work in progress and finished goods.
- Aged debtors.
- Aged creditors.

All cash transactions should be recorded immediately. Exercise daily cash control; all cheques and cash should be paid into the bank on the day they are received. Any cash in hand, in excess of short-term requirements, should be placed in an interest-bearing account. For all but the very smallest business it will help monitoring considerably if you maintain a sales ledger and purchase ledger so that assets and liabilities can be quickly calculated. You need to have the information as quickly as possible. It is better to have 80 per cent of the data immediately than 100 per cent when it is too late to use. Try not to generate too much or you will find it difficult to use. One business that I know simply generates a list of aged debtors every week and keeps chasing them to pay. They find this a particularly helpful form of control and all that they require.

127

Turning the data into graphs, tables and charts can help by revealing trends, which in turn helps in the revision of forecasts and future planning. Modern computer spreadsheets have extremely good graphics and are very effective in this role.

Statutory requirements

Each year the Inland Revenue will want to know how much profit your business made in its previous year in order to assess the business for the tax due. If you do not supply accounts showing how much your business made then the Inland Revenue will estimate the profit they think the business has made and assess you accordingly. This could lead to a demand for more tax than you should be paying. It is important not to under-disclose sales of the business, for example, by netting off payments, as the Inland Revenue will charge penalties and interest on any tax not paid at the correct time. They have techniques based on the analysis of similar types of business which enable them to check whether it is likely that sales have been made for cash and not included in the figures shown in the accounts.

If you employ staff, you must deduct their income tax and national insurance under the pay as you earn (PAYE) scheme and send it to the Inland Revenue regularly. They also insist on the way that records relating to wages and tax are kept.

If you are registered for VAT, as many businesses are, then the VAT regulations require you to keep accounts and that the VAT element is shown separately in those accounts. A quarterly return must then be provided to the VAT inspectors. There are considerable penalties for late payment but preparing the VAT return is simple and straightforward provided all the figures are recorded in your book-keeping system.

If your business is incorporated (i.e. it is a company) and has a turnover exceeding £90,000 then you must have your accounts audited every year by a registered auditor. These must then be filed at Companies House. Small businesses can, however, file an abbreviated form of account instead of the full accounts, though they still have to prepare full accounts for shareholders and for the Inland Revenue. Once accounts are filed, they are in the public domain. You would probably choose, therefore, to file modified accounts in order not to give away too much about your business.

Book-keeping

Since the purpose of this book is to look at financial control, not book-keeping, we will look briefly at a simple single entry book-keeping system based on the use of cash analysis books and then briefly at double entry book-keeping. There are a number of proprietary cash book systems available (e.g. Simplex, Guildhall, Finco, Kalamazoo, etc). They are all designed to simplify the book-keeping process as much as possible. However, it is important to understand the principles of book-keeping if the figures are going to be useful in providing effective control. To keep adequate records, you need books of account as follows:

- Cash book.
- Sales ledger.
- Purchase ledger.
- Wages book.
- Petty cash book.
- Stock book.

Of these, the cash book is most essential as it keeps track of all payments and receipts and can be used to perform regular reconciliation with the bank statements.

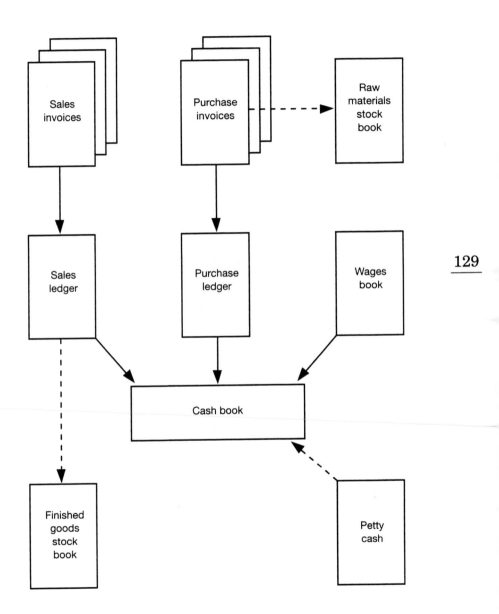

Figure 8.1 Simple book-keeping system

Receipts

Date	Name	Ref	Bank	VAT	Sales	Other
	Brought forward		1000.00			
1/6	R Fox & Co	300	2350.00	350.00	2000.00	
8/6	Bracewell	301	822.50	122.50	700.00	
11/6	Beardsley Ltd	302	4112.50	612.50	3500.00	
18/6	S.Watson	303	587.50	87.50	500.00	
20/6	Kitsons	304	470.00	70.00	400.00	
21/6	Bank interest	statement	70.00			70.00
23/6	McDermott	305	235.00	35.00	200.00	
23/6	Keegan Ltd	305	117.50	17.50	100.00	
28/6	Hall	306	4700.00	700.00	4000.00	
29/6	Cash sales	307	117.50	17.50	100.00	
Totals			13582.50	2012.50	11500.00	70.00
Monthly movement			875.00			
Balance carried forward			1875.00			

Payments

Date	Details	Chq	Bank	VAT	Materials	Travel	Premises	Capital	Wages	Petty cash	Other
1/6	Smicek Ltd	523	587.50	87.50	500.00						
1/6	M.Hottiger	524	705.00	105.00	600.00						
2/6	Peacock Property	525	1000.00				1000.00				
8/6	Petty Cash	526	100.00							100.00	
10/6	S.Howey plc	527	470.00	70.00							400.00
13/6	Beresford Autos	528	117.50	17.50		100.00					
14/6	Venison Plant	529	2350.00	350.00				2000.00			
17/6	Inland Revenue	530	2000.00						2000.00		
18/6	K Gillespie	531	25.00								25.00
20/6	Wages	a/pay	5000.00						5000.00		
29/6	Lee Ltd	532	352.50	52.50	300.00						
Totals			12707.50	682.50	1400.00	100.00	1000.00	2000.00	7000.00	100.00	425.00

Single entry book-keeping

Cash book

Look at the figure opposite which shows a typical cash book layout. An analysis book should be used which has a number of columns across the page. The number and headings of the columns will depend on the categories of receipts and payments which are likely to be incurred regularly. It is conventional for receipts to be recorded on the left-hand page and payments on the right-hand page. Personally, I arrange my analysis books so that one line goes across the double page spread with one entry per line, as I find this easier to read. This can be particularly helpful if you have more than one bank account, say a current account and a deposit account, as transfers are then shown on the same line on both pages.

This example assumes that the cash book is being used to record all the transactions of the business and that there is no sales or purchase ledger in use.

Every time a cheque is received or issued, the total amount should be entered in the column headed 'bank' on the relevant page and then analysed into the appropriate columns. This immediate analysis enables you to monitor the major and the most important items. On the payments side, you would certainly expect to include raw materials, wages, premises costs and capital costs. You would probably choose other headings depending on the likely areas of expenditure by your business. Payments made by standing order or direct debit should also be recorded. Note in the example, the payment for wages which has not been by cheque, but by credit transfer from the business's bank account direct to its employees' bank accounts. At the end of the month all the columns should be totalled. The sum of the separate totals should equal the addition of the total (i.e. the bank) column. At the end of each month deduct the expenditure from the income to give the net cashflow for the month. Then add the figure carried forward from the previous month to give the carry down figure. As you would expect, this is also the balance that should be in the bank. If the figure is positive – i.e. you have money in the bank – it is carried forward to the next receipts page, as shown in the example. If the figure is negative – i.e. you have an overdraft – it is carried forward on to the next payments page.

The cash book should exactly represent every movement on the bank account. At the end of each month, you should reconcile the cash book with your bank statement. This is a means of ensuring that the cash book and statements do agree as well as ensuring that you remain within your agreed overdraft facility if you have one. If your cash flow

131

is particularly tight you may need to do reconciliations as often as daily to stay within agreed overdraft limits.

Midland Bank plc

BOB'S BUILDERS LIMITED

77 GRAINGER STREET
NEWCASTLE NE99 1SA TEL 0912325792

Statement of Account

1995	Sheet 19	Y Account No. 81284669	DEBIT	CREDIT	BALANCE Credit C Debit D	
02-JUNE	BALANCE BROUGHT FORWARD				1000.00	C
02-JUN	SUNDRIES	200300		2350.00	3350.00	C
04-JUN		100523	587.50		2762.50	C
04-JUN		100524	705.00		2057.50	C
08-JUN	SUNDRIES	200301		822.50	2880.00	C
08-JUN		100526	100.00		2780.00	C
10-JUN		100525	1000.00		1780.00	C
11-JUN	SUNDRIES	200302		4112.50	5892.50	C
18-JUN	SUNDRIES	200303		587.50	6480.00	C
19-JUN		100529	2350.00		4130.00	C
19-JUN		100527	470.00		3660.00	C
19-JUN		100528	117.50		3542.50	C
20-JUN		100530	2000.00		1542.50	C
20-JUN	WAGES		5000.00		- 3457.50	D
21-JUN	SUNDRIES	200304		470.00	- 2987.50	D
21-JUN	INTEREST			70.00	- 2917.50	D
23-JUN		200305		352.50	- 2565.00	D
24-JUN		100531	25.00		- 2590.00	D

Figure 8.2   Bank statement

Look at the bank statement in Figure 8.2. If there are additional items, such as bank charges, interest, standing orders, etc., then these should be recorded in the cash book as with the interest received amount shown in Figure 8.1. As you can see, all the transactions in the cash book have been recorded except three that occurred too late in the month. These are the cheque issued to Lee Ltd and the cheque received from Hall. In addition, the receipt for the cash sale had not been banked by the end of the month. You should reconcile the figures by taking the bank balance you have calculated from your records, deducting uncleared receipts and adding back uncleared payments. This should give the statement balance. If it does not, then you have an error somewhere.

Book balance	1875.00
less: uncleared receipts	(4817.50)
plus: unpresented payments	352.50
Bank statement balance	(2590.00)

Note that the cash book is showing a positive balance, but that there is actually an overdraft at the bank. It is important to watch the timing of payments in order not to become more overdrawn than you would like. Even if your cash flow forecast shows a positive balance at the end of every month, there may be occasions during the month when this problem might arise.

The sales ledger

The sales ledger records the sales for the month, the amount of cash received and shows what is currently due to the business. Every time an invoice is issued it should be recorded in the sales ledger. A copy of the invoice should be retained, showing the details of the work for which the invoice has been issued, a unique invoice number, your VAT registration number, the VAT rate and the amount of VAT. A typical format for a sales ledger is shown below. As can be seen, there is a column to enter the date when an invoice is paid. It is thus extremely easy to see which invoices are outstanding so as to chase them. You may also find it helpful to add up the outstanding debtors at the end of each month and make a note of the figure. Compare the invoices paid in June with the cash book example on page 130.

133

Sales Ledger						
Invoice date	Customer	Inv. no.	Gross amount	VAT	Net sales	Date paid
1/5	Bracewell	9001	822.50	122.50	700.00	8/6
3/5	R. Fox & Co	9002	2350.00	350.00	2000.00	3/6
4/5	Beardsley Ltd	9003	4112.50	612.50	3500.00	11/6
8/5	Kitsons	9004	470.00	70.00	400.00	20/6
10/5	McDermott	9005	235.00	35.00	200.00	23/6
15/6	Beardsley Ltd	9006	2350.00	350.00	2000.00	
20/5	S. Watson	9007	587.50	87.50	500.00	18/6
28/5	Albert plc	9008	1175.00	175.00	1000.00	
31/5	Hall	9009	4700.00	700.00	4000.00	28/6
Total			16802.50	2502.50		
Debtors outstanding			3525.00			

If desired, more than one column can be used for sales to analyse sales into different categories.

This format will also satisfy the requirements for accounting for VAT.

The purchase ledger

Many people are more cavalier with bills (i.e. purchase invoices) often tossing them in a desk drawer until the end of the month. While this is simple, it is bad practice. You do not know how much you owe to your suppliers or even whether you still have all the bills – some are sure to get mislaid resulting in unpaid and, therefore, upset suppliers and more importantly potential legal action which could have a detrimental effect on your future ability to obtain credit.

The purchase ledger works in a similar manner to the sales ledger and is used to record all suppliers' invoices and to show those which are still unpaid (and allow VAT to be accounted for). A similar format to the payments side of the cash book is generally used, though it excludes columns, such as wages, for which you do not receive bills. Once again, you may find it helpful to add up the outstanding creditors at the end of each month and make a note of the figure.

Purchase Ledger									
Date	Supplier	Ref. no.	Gross	VAT	Materials	Marketing	Premises	Capital	Date paid
1/5	Srineck Ltd	900	235.00	35.00	200.00				1/6
2/5	S.Howey plc	901	470.00	70.00		400.00			10/6
8/5	Srineck Ltd	902	352.50	52.50	300.00				1/6
20/5	Venison Plant	903	2350.00	350.00				200.00	14/6
21/5	Lee Ltd	904	352.00	52.50	300.00				29/6
23/5	M Hottiger	905	705.00	105.00	600.00				1/6
27/5	L.Clark	906	1175.00	175.00	1000.00				
28/5	Peacock Property	907	1000.00				1000.00		2/6
Total			6640.00	840.00	2400.00	400.00	1000.00	2000.00	
Creditors outstanding			1175.00						

As with the sales ledger, the VAT figures can be quickly extracted when required.

While it is not essential to use purchase order numbers, it makes good sense. If you use a purchase ledger, you will be able to number the bills as they are received and record the number in the ledger so that you can easily retrieve the bill if a query arises later.

If you are placing orders for goods to be received at some date in the future, then you should give an order number. If you are likely to have a lot of goods on order at any time, then set up an order book so that you can quickly see the level of your commitment. Allocate unique numbers and use order forms. Cross referencing is important to provide an audit trail. Write the cheque number on purchase invoices as well as in the cash book or purchase ledger. File in order by cheque number. If you do not place many orders then you may think this is undesirably bureaucratic. Do not be like one business, known to the author, who made up order numbers by reversing the six digits of the date and adding four extra digits chosen at random.

If sales or purchase ledgers are being used then any receipts or payments in respect of invoices recorded through these ledgers need not be analysed in the cash books as this analysis will be performed in the relevant ledger. These transactions should be recorded in the cash book under a column titled debtors (for receipts) or creditors (for payments) as shown in the figure opposite. Other receipts and payments will still have to be analysed however.

Receipts

Date	Name	Ref	Bank	VAT	Debtor ledger	Sales	Other
	Brought forward		1000.00				
3/6	R Fox & Co	300	2350.00		2350.00		
8/6	Bracewell	301	822.50		822.50		
1/6	Beardsley	302	4112.50		4112.50		
8/6	Watson	303	587.50		587.50		
0/6	Kitson	304	470.00		470.00		
1/6	Interest	Statement	70.00				70.00
3/6	McDermott	305	235.00		235.00		
3/6	Keegan	305	117.50		117.50		
8/6	Hall	306	4700.00		4700.00		
9/6	Cash Sales	307	117.50	17.50		100.00	
	Totals		13582.50	17.50	13395.00	100.00	70.00

Payments

Date	Details	Chq	Bank	VAT	Creditor Ledger	Travel	Wages	Petty cash	Other
1/6	Smicek Ltd	523	587.50		587.50				
1/6	Hottiger	524	705.00		705.00				
2/6	Peacock	525	1000.00		1000.00				
8/6	Petty cash	526	100.00					100.00	
10/6	Howey	527	470.00		470.00				
13/6	Beresford	528	117.50	17.50		100.00			
14/6	Venison	529	2350.00		2350.00				
17/6	Inland Revenue	530	2000.00				2000.00		
18/6	Gillespie	531	25.00						25.00
20/6	Wages	a/pay	5000.00				5000.00		
29/6	Lee	532	352.50		325.50				
	Totals		12707.50	17.50	5465.00	100.00	7000.00	100.00	25.00

Double entry book-keeping

Many people insist on the desirability of double entry book-keeping. The principles of double entry were first put forward over 500 years ago by Luca Pacioli, a Franciscan monk, and are fairly simple. The basic principle is that each transaction is recorded in two (or more) accounts as a debit (left side) and a credit (right side). The total debit entry is equal to the total credit entry and as such the system is self balancing, thus making the search for errors easier. Trial balances can quickly be determined by summarising the balance from each account.

Debit (+)	Credit (-)
Incoming asset or cost	Outgoing asset or income

You'll notice that the use of T accounts and the descriptions are similar to the sources and applications of funds described in Chapter 2. This section is not intended to teach you how to do double entry book-keeping, but simply to introduce you to the principles involved, since all computerised accounting systems are based on double entry principles.

Let's work through a simple example. Simon designs, manufactures and distributes shirts. He starts with £20,000 which he introduces into the business as capital. This is shown as a credit in the capital account and as a debit in the cash account (transaction a).

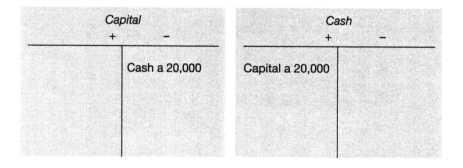

He borrows a further £20,000 from the bank which is shown in a loan account and in the cash account (transaction b).

Loan			Cash	
+	−		+	−
	Cash b 20,000		Capital a 20,000	
			Loan b 20,000	
			40,000	

He buys some machinery which costs £15,000 (transaction c). To avoid the added complication at this stage of sales and purchases on credit all transactions are assumed to be for cash.

Machinery			Cash	
+	−		+	−
Cash c 15,000			Capital a 20,000	M/c c 15,000
			Loan b 20,000	
			40,000	15,000

He buys raw materials costing £5,000 (transaction d).

Raw materials			Cash	
+	−		+	−
Cash d 15,000			Capital a 20,000	M/c c 15,000
			Loan b 20,000	Matl d 5,000
			40,000	20,000

During his first month, Simon turns materials worth £3,000 (e) into shirts all of which he sells. This leaves him with £2,000 worth of stock for his second month's production.

Raw materials					Direct costs			
+		−			+		−	
Cash d	5,000	DC	e	3,000	Matl	e	3,000	
	5,000			3,000				

He incurs overhead costs of £3,000 (transaction f).

Overheads			Cash			
+		−	+		−	
Cash f	3,000		Capital a 20,000		M/c c	15,000
			Capital b 20,000		Matl d	5,000
					Exp f	3,000
			40,000			23,000

His sales generate income of £7,500 (transaction g).

Sales			Cash			
+		−	+		−	
		Cash g 7,500	Capital a 20,000		M/c c	15,000
			Capital b 20,000		Matl d	5,000
			Sales g 7,500		Exp e	3,000
			47,500			23,000

It is now possible to prepare a trial balance which is simply the sum of the balances from all of the T charts.

Account	Debit	Credit
Capital		20,000
Loan		20,000
Machinery	15,000	
Raw materials	2,000	
Overheads	3,000	
Direct costs	3,000	
Sales		7,500
Cash	24,500	
Balances	47,500	47,500

If the balance figures for each of debit and credit are different, then you have made a mistake. Once the trial balance has been prepared, it is relatively straightforward to prepare the profit and loss account and the balance sheet.

Profit & loss account		
Sales		7,500
Direct costs	2,000	
Overheads	3,000	
Net profit (balancing figure)	2,500	
		7,500

Balance sheet				
Finance		Assets		
Owner's capital	20,000	Machinery	15,000	
Loan	20,000	Stock	3,000	
Profit	2,500	Cash	24,500	
	42,500		42,500	

Stock control

Stock is normally valued in the balance sheet at cost or net realisable value, whichever is the lower. Net realisable value is the amount of money you might receive if you were forced to sell quickly. It is reasonable to assume raw materials (e.g. wood, flour, electronic components) could be resold for the sum at which they were bought. But half-completed work in progress may only have scrap value. If you are trading, you may get caught out by changes in price or new models being introduced by the manufacturer, frequently seen in computing for example.

Catherine's Chairs: Raw materials stock record		Materials received	Issued to production	Stock remaining
	Opening stock		1,000	1,000
1/7				0
3/7	Willy's Wood	2,000		2,000
8/7			1,000	1,000
15/7			1,000	0
18/7	Tim's Timber	2,000		2,000
22/7			1,400	600
29/7			400	200
	Total	4,000	4,800	200

As raw materials are received, they are recorded. As raw materials are issued to production, they are also recorded. For the sake of simplicity, we will value work in progress and finished goods only as the cost of materials.

Catherine's Chairs: Work in progress record

		Materials to production	Goods finished	WIP remaining
	Opening stock			0
1/7		1,000		1,000
7/7			800	200
8/7		1,000		1,200
14/7			800	400
15/7		1,000		1,400
21/7			1,200	200
22/7		1,400		1,600
28/7			1,400	200
29/7		400		600
31/7			400	200
	Total	4,800	4,600	200

When goods are finished, they cease to be work in progress and become finished goods stock. As they are dispatched, they are deducted from the total finished goods stock.

Catherine's Chairs: Finished goods record

		Goods completed	Goods dispatched	Goods remaining
	Opening stock			0
7/7		800		800
9/7	Andy's Arcade		100	700
11/7	Furniture by Fiona		300	400
13/7	Brian's Bazaar		200	200
14/7		800		1,000
15/7	Amanda's Artefacts		300	700
18/7	Tracy Trading Inc		400	300
21/7		1,200		1,500
23/7	Absoultely Pat		500	1,000
25/7	Sonya's Supplies		600	400
28/7		1,400		1,800
29/7	Kim's Kreations		500	1,300
30/7	Creature Comforts		1,300	0
31/7		400		400
	Total	4,600	4,200	400

If you take care to record raw materials as they progess through work in progress to completed goods and then to dispatch and invoice it will be easy to identify stock holdingss. In Catherine's case:

Raw materials	200
WIP	200
Finished goods	400
Total stock	800

If you have a service business, or only use low levels of raw materials, then you can dispense with the stock control records. If raw material stock is used in more than one product then you need to allocate the cost of those materials when they are released to manufacture. By the time that you have grown that large, you will probably have introduced a computerised book-keeping system with a stock control facility. If you are retailing, you will probably just record everything together since otherwise the records would become too unwieldy, and without a clever till it would be impossible to record individual items as they are sold.

141

The wages book

When you start to employ people, you should inform the Inland Revenue who will provide a very comprehensive pack with forms for recording payments and deductions for each employee and instructions on their use. It is not essential to have a wages book in addition since it only records the same information. However, the payments and deductions for all employees for each week or month will be summarised together if you do use one. Wages books are designed for recording wages and deductions and show the break down of the total wages paid by a business in any week or month. They record the following details for each employee:

- Gross pay.
- Employee's National Insurance contributions.
- Pension and/or other deductions.
- Net pay.
- Employer's National Insurance and pension contributions.

Since the calculations are routine and tedious, payroll lends itself extremely easily to being computerised, with the further advantage that you can immediately print payslips, autopay lists, monthly and year-to-date summaries, etc. The principles of PAYE are exactly the same for every business and there are some excellent computerised payroll packages around such as Sage and Pegasus. Figure 8.3 shows a typical screen from Sage[1] – this one illustrates current and year to date figures for an individual employee. Figure 8.4 illustrates the payslip for an individual employee. Entering the weekly or monthly pay is done via a screen and is, therefore, very straightforward.

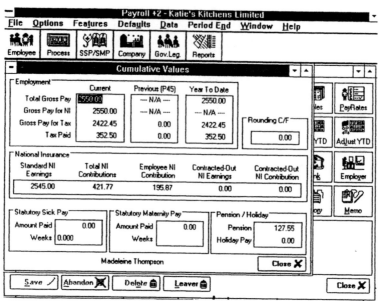

Figure 8.3   Employee's detailed record on screen

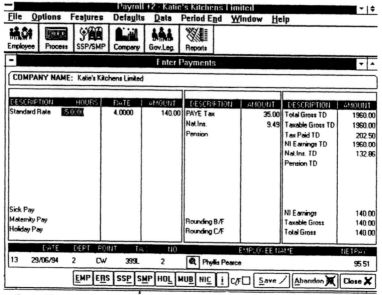

Figure 8.4   Employee's payslip

[1] The computer illustrations are from Sage Sterling 2 for Windows.

The wages book will not be described any further here. The net wage payments and the payments of tax and NI must be transferred to the cash book when the cheques are issued. Note that these are not payments that would be recorded in the purchase ledger since they are not purchases. Once you start to employ several staff you might find it helpful to use one of the special schemes operated by the banks such as 'Autopay' operated by Nat West Bank. With Autopay you simply send one form to the bank with all the net payments listed. The bank then automatically credits your employees' accounts on the day you say and debits your account accordingly.

The petty cash book

Most businesses will require to have some cash available, for example, to buy stamps, coffee, etc. Cash kept on the premises should, of course, be locked away. Payments in cash also need to be recorded. The petty cash book will show all cash receipts and payments in a similar format to the cash book and analysed similarly. Amounts shown as received in the petty cash book should match the amounts in the petty cash column on the payments page of the cash book, i.e. when a cheque is cashed. The amount of cash in the petty cash box at any time should equal the balance shown by the petty cash book.

143

Accounting records for cash businesses

Some businesses – for example, retail – deal almost entirely in cash on the sale of their goods rather than invoicing and awaiting payment at a later date. Clearly, they can simplify their accounting procedures. A retail business would total up the entire amount of cash taken, say, each day. This would be paid into the bank and simply shown on the receipts side of the cash book as, for example 'Tuesday's takings'.

Many businesses which receive large amounts of money as cash also tend, however, to use some of that cash to pay bills (and reduce their bank charges). Clearly, you cannot simply take money out of the till without recording it. These payments also need to be recorded in the main cash book. One possibility is to have two books, one which covers all cheque transactions and one which covers all cash transactions (though this is obviously more important than the petty cash book described above). When cash is paid into the bank, or when a cheque is cashed to provide money, say, for the float, then an entry has to be made in both books. An alternative, however, is to add a 'cash' column after the 'bank' column in the cash analysis book. Receipts and payments are then shown either in the bank column or in the cash column

– but not both. They are then analysed into the appropriate columns. Transfers between bank and cash are thus shown on both pages, but otherwise the book is kept exactly as described above. If you choose to use one line per entry across the double page spread, you would enter both halves of the transfer on the same line. You would do the same if you have more than one bank account, say, a current account and an interest bearing deposit account.

When you have only a bank column, the total received will eventually equal the total income to the business – when all the debts are paid – and it is the same for the expenditure. If you have a bank column and a cash column, however, do not make the mistake of adding the two together to tell you your income or expenditure. Because of the transfers, they simply show cash moving around the system. You need to use the appropriate analysis columns instead.

Allocating income and expenditure

144

As will be apparent from the above, there is nothing particularly complicated about recording all the data relating to sales and purchases and to receipts and payments. If you produce more than one product or service, however, you will want to be able to attribute sales and purchases to the appropriate product.

Overhead costs can be allocated between products as described in Chapter 5 for costing purposes and would be recorded without any attempt at splitting. The direct costs, however, do need to be allocated. If you only have a small choice of products then one simple way to do this is to have a separate column for each product or service both in the sales ledger and in the purchase ledger. Remember it is the sales and purchase figures that are relevant, not the receipts and expenses. These figures can be recorded in the cash book as described earlier with no need to distinguish them. If you have several products and this method is impractical, you may choose to have a separate sales ledger and a separate purchases ledger for each product. You will then need to have an additional purchases ledger for those overheads not directly attributable to a particular product. This separation is, however, very easy to do if you computerise your accounts.

Computerising your accounts

Most computerised accounting packages such as Sage, Pegasus or TAS include fully integrated sales, purchases and nominal ledgers (i.e. an entry in the sales or purchase ledger automatically updates the nomi-

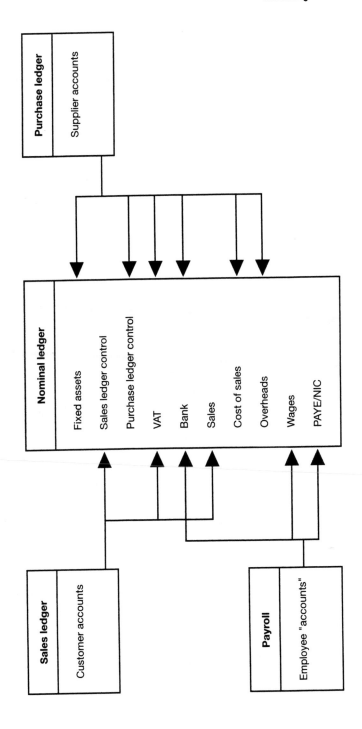

Figure 8.5   Intergrated ledger system

nal ledger also). Optional add-ons which may or may not be integrated include payroll, order processing, stock control and job costing, forecasting facilities, ratio analysis and variance analysis.

As already noted, it is important to understand the basic principles of book-keeping and double entry before computerising your management information system. A good system can increase the speed at which information is produced but the output is only as good as the information that is entered. Before purchasing a system consider the functions you require and compare those available on different packages. Strictly, the agreement of your local VAT office should be sought before computerising as they will require assurance that the details described for a manual system and a full audit trail are present. Once the system is purchased, follow the instructions in the documentation carefully, as errors in installation and setting up are often the most difficult to correct.

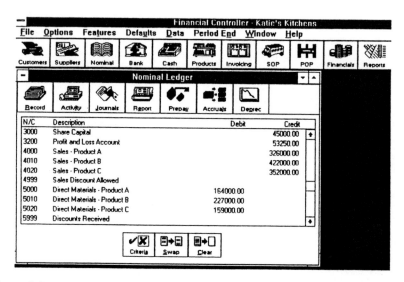

Figure 8.6　Nominal ledger record

All customer, supplier and nominal ledger (asset, liability, income and expense) accounts will need to be coded. When doing so, consider the structure of your required management reports and structure your coding accordingly. It is suggested, for example, that intervals are left between account codes when setting up so that a new sales type, say, could be added next to the existing sales type. With no intervals this could not be done and the logic of the accounts structure would be lost. Figure 8.6 taken from the nominal ledger of Sage Financial Controller shows the intervals between codes.

You will need to code everything; all your sales and all your expenditure. Look back at your last few months' records to see what could usefully be coded separately. Be as logical as possible. While it is always possible to add extra codes later, you may eventually lose the initial logical layout.

Entering the data

Rather than entering every sales or purchase invoice immediately it arrives, I would suggest that you collect them together. They can then be entered as a batch, say, daily or weekly. However, you should not use this as an excuse not to enter the data regularly, or this will reduce the accuracy of the management information available. The illustrations below are also from Sage Financial Controller and show some of the figures from Katie's Kitchens. They are simply intended to give a feel for an accounting package, not to show you how to do it all!

Figure 8.7 shows the list of customers with their outstanding balances.

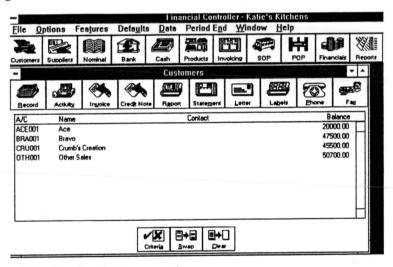

Figure 8.7   Nominal ledger record

Figure 8.8 shows a customer invoice. It is easy to complete and, once saved, posts the entries to the correct ledgers automatically. It can also be printed to send to your customer.

When invoices are received from suppliers they can be entered into the systems purchase ledger, showing what was bought from whom and when. Once again, when this is saved the figures are automatically posted to the correct ledgers.

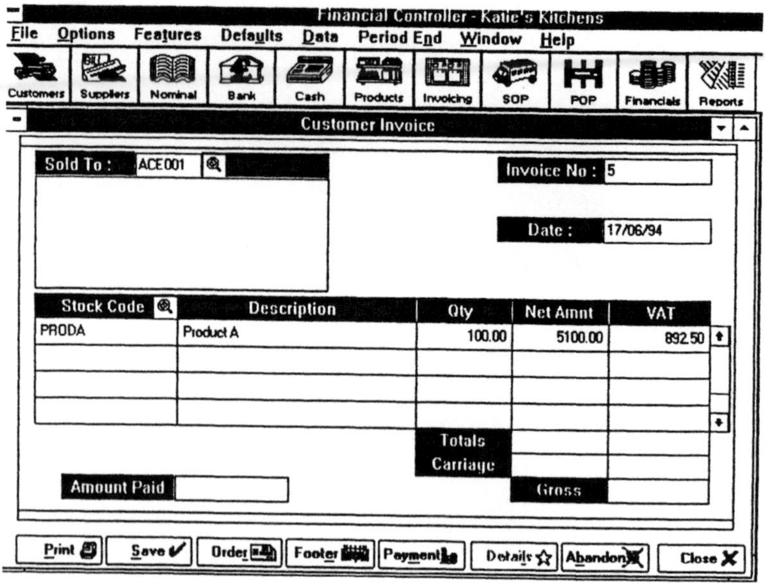

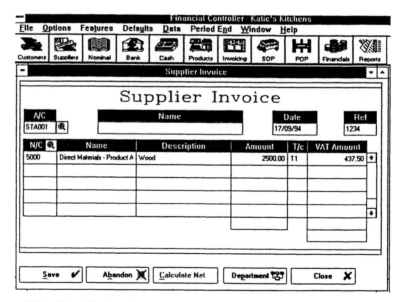

Figure 8.8　Customer invoice

Figure 8.9　Supplier invoice

The importance of bank reconciliation was explained earlier. This is also very easy with a computer system. The items can be compared with the bank statement and checked off. The computer calculates the statement balance at all times so it is very easy to see if you have an error anywhere.

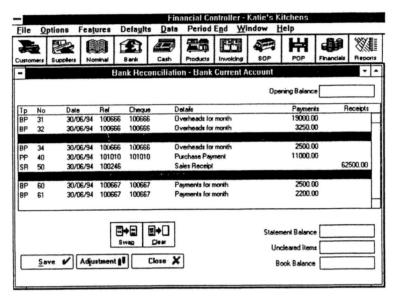

Figure 8.10 **Bank reconciliation**

You will need to take care that entries are properly coded, that the data is entered only once, that they are entered into the correct ledger and that the figures are arithmetically correct. While safeguards and validation checks are usually built into the software, it is still possible to enter data incorrectly, which will then affect all the figures. If errors are made, then do refer to the documentation to ensure that the corrections are made properly. If, for example, a sales invoice is issued twice, then a credit note needs to be entered through the sales ledger rather than simply correcting the cash book.

You will probably find it helpful to consult with your accountant, business advisor or enterprise agency when computerising your accounts. They will almost certainly have experience of a range of software and will be able to advise on the most appropriate software for your business. Furthermore, they will probably be able to help you set it up in a way that is not only simple for you to use, but also helps them to do their job at the end of each year.

The VAT return

If your turnover is below £350,000 you may account for output VAT on an invoice basis (i.e. what you have invoiced) or on a cash basis (i.e.

149

what you have actually received). If your turnover is over £350,000 you must account for output VAT on an invoice basis. You may account for input VAT on a purchase basis (i.e. whether or not you have paid for goods) or on a cash basis. Whichever method you choose, the figures are quickly available from the sales and purchase ledgers or from the cash books if you follow the simple suggestions made earlier.

The relevant figures can then be easily transferred to the quarterly VAT return. If your turnover is below £300,000 you may complete an annual return, which has both administrative and cash-flow benefits. For VAT purposes, expenditure includes payments to suppliers that are zero rated or exempt from VAT, but excludes VAT, wages, tax, loan repayments, etc. Your VAT return will look like the facsimile which Sage uses in its software and which is shown in Figure 8.11.

150

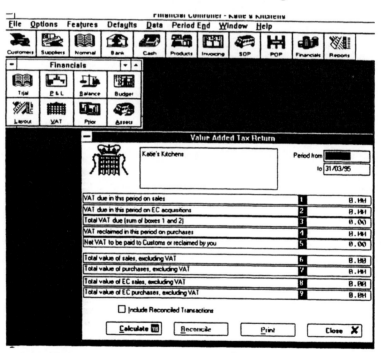

Figure 8.11   Record of VAT return

There are a number of specific rules for some activities, such as the construction industry. Retailers normally operate a retail scheme to take care of the fact that some goods may be standard rated and some zero rated. If you are in any doubt, then contact your nearest VAT office.

Monthly check

Accounting records, if properly maintained, can be used on a day-to-day basis to see how a business is doing. At least monthly, there are a number of tasks which must be done carefully. Ensure you bring the cash book up to date and carry out a bank reconciliation. The cash book may need to be updated for any omitted entries such as standing orders or bank charges. The cash book balance represents the business's liquidity – it is the cash immediately available to the business.

Reconciliation should be done at the end of every month. The balance in the cash book is likely to differ from the balance on the bank statement due to time-lags but the difference should be reconciled as shown earlier.

Good financial software will enable you to input your annual budget on a monthly basis, and also retain your previous year's actual performance for comparison. Each month, after you have input the actual figures, the software will be able to produce monthly and year to date profit and loss accounts and balance sheets and a variance analysis. Even if you have not computerised your book-keeping you should still compare the actual cash-flow figures with the budgeted figures. That is why many cash-flow forecast forms have columns for both forecast and actual.

151

Conclusion and checklist

Collecting the right information is a vital prerequisite for monitoring and controlling any business's finances.

Every accountant seems to have the client whose accounting system is two shoe boxes – one for invoices issued and one for bills received – which the accountant is then given at the end of the year and expected to turn into sensible accounts. You will have an effective book-keeping system if:

- You record every transaction promptly (or at least by the end of the day);
- You maintain a sales ledger and a purchase ledger in addition to the main cash book; and
- You are able to derive key information quickly and easily.

You should set up a book-keeping system which includes the following:

- Cash book;
- Sales ledger;
- Purchase ledger;
- Wages book;
- Petty cash book;
- Stock book (if appropriate).

The system should be able to give the following information simply and easily at any time:

- Cash position;
- Outstanding debtors;
- Outstanding creditors.

You should quickly be able to devise a profit and loss account and a balance sheet from the figures. This is essential if you are going to keep a close eye on profitability and if you are going to keep all the costs under tight control. Quite apart from the need to know the financial position of the business in order to manage it effectively, there is also a requirement imposed by outsiders. Customs and Excise can impose fines and interest for late submission of or for errors in your VAT returns. The Registrar of Companies can impose fines for late submission of company accounts. The Inland Revenue can impose penal interest for late payment of personal or corporation tax.

Accounting software is so cheap these days that, if you have a computer, it makes a great deal of sense to computerise your book-keeping tasks. The software will then do all the hard work for you – though you still need to look carefully at the figures, understand what they are telling you and then exercise appropriate control. This is the topic of the next chapter.

9

Keeping track of the figures

If your financial control is going to be effective you need regularly to analyse your actual performance figures and compare them both against the plan and, perhaps, against your performance historically.

- **One easy way of comparing actuals and budgets is through variance analysis.**
- **Usually, only a few figures need to be watched regularly to achieve effective control.**
- **Using a computer based spreadsheet will assist with all your analysis requirements.**

Management Information Systems

Having a suitable management information system (MIS) is a prerequisite for effective monitoring. Although it might sound daunting, an MIS can be extremely simple. An MIS is simply a set of procedures set up by you and your staff to ensure that data about the business is collected, recorded, reported and evaluated quickly and efficiently. That information is then used to check the progress of the business and to control it effectively. For most small businesses, there are likely only to be a few key elements.

- *Marketing monitoring* – Are you achieving your sales targets measured both by level of sales and market share? How full is your order book? Are customers paying the right price?
- *Production* – How does the level of output compare with the level of sales? What is the percentage of rejects? How does the actual cost compare with the budgeted cost?
- *Staff monitoring* – Are the staff being effective? Are they satisfied and motivated?
- *Financial control* – Are you meeting your financial targets?

You will need to ensure that you have proper systems in place to ensure that

- You keep careful track of everything bought by the business, especially if the person ordering is not the person who pays the bills.
- You record everything sold by the business and that everything is properly invoiced, especially if the person doing the selling is not the person who raises the invoices or chases customers for payment.
- There is an effective stock control system which records incoming raw materials and compares them against purchase orders, monitors progress through the production stages if appropriate and records the dispatch of finished goods.
- All payments and receipts are recorded to ensure that bank balances and overdraft limits are kept within agreed levels.

Computerised accounting packages and spreadsheets make it relatively straightforward to record data and present it in a format which is easily understood. It still requires discipline to ensure that the data is collected, but making an effort will be rewarded through the improved understanding that you will have of your business. Earlier, we covered a wide range of figures and ratios that it is possible to monitor – and there are many others.

> The key to an effective management information system is to ensure that you only monitor a small number of figures and that those figures are related back to the strategic objectives and the operational objectives that you have set for your business.

If other people need to see the figures, then ensure that they get them speedily. If your system of financial control is to be successful, you need to have the figures quickly available after the end of each month.

Watching your sales

All the figures need to be watched closely, but some, such as cash flow, aged debtors or sales variances, need to be watched frequently; others, such as capital expenditure or labour turnover, while still important, can be reviewed less frequently. Arguably, the most important figure to watch is your sales figure. Although, as we will see in a moment, simply achieving your sales target is insufficient by itself. Failing to achieve at least your break-even sales will, ultimately, be catastrophic for the business.

154

It was suggested earlier that you prepare a graph showing cumulative monthly sales target and cumulative monthly break-even sales against time. As the year progresses, then you can plot your actual sales on the sales graph. If you do not achieve your targets you will need to take remedial action. But even if you do achieve your sales target by value, there may be hidden problems. These can, however, be easily discovered if you analyse all the figures carefully.

Cumulative sales target

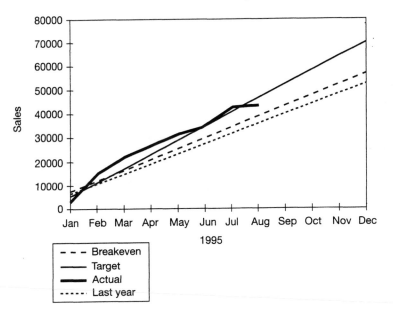

155

Variance analysis

Provided you are keeping your books accurately, it should be possible at any time, and at least monthly, to generate a comprehensive financial picture of how the business is doing. You can then look at the *variances*.

A variance is simply the difference between your target and your actual performance. Variance analysis looks at the differences themselves, rather than comparing them with one another as in ratio analysis.

Whether variances are positive or negative, they will have implications for your business. As was explained earlier, the costing and pricing system for your business is based on estimating future costs. It is essential, therefore, to monitor actual costs against budgeted costs to ensure that you are on track.

Many businesses fail because action has not been taken to rectify problems that variance analysis would have highlighted. Review the variances regularly, at least once per month, after you have balanced the books. For each difference, ask what caused it. Watch for variances simply caused by differences in timing – have orders been brought forward or delayed? How accurate are your budgeted figures? If sales are below budget, was the budget over-optimistic? Can the business survive on the lower levels of sales? Can you compensate by an increase in price? Or will a price decrease generate more sales? Are you spending too much on raw materials? Can you find cheaper suppliers? Can you reduce overheads? Can you become more productive?

156

To be effective, analysing variances has to consider more than just differences in cash. Indeed, there may be major variances even though the overall cash position remains more or less as forecast. The following figures should be reviewed regularly:

- Sales, enquiry and order position
- Material and labour usage
- Overheads
- Cash position/cash forecast
- Stock
- Capital expenditure.

The next few paragraphs are designed to help you keep track of variances within your own business. We will once again use Katie's Kitchen as an example.

Sales variances

As you might guess, you should monitor the sales for each product both by volume and by value either of which might vary. A sales variance therefore comprises two parts: a sales price variance and a sales volume variance. If your price drops but your volume increases this may give a favourable sales variance, depending on the respective changes.

The tables below show one way of monitoring sales by volume and by value both on a monthly and a cumulative basis. The figures for the corresponding period last year enable you also to see at a glance how you are doing compared to last year's sales figures.

Sales by volume (month six)

	Month			Year to date			Last year
	Budget	*Actual*	*Variance*	*Budget*	*Actual*	*Variance*	*Month*
Product A	300	294	(6)	1,800	1,294	(506)	300
Product B	110	117	7	660	833	173	88
Product C	100	110	10	600	450	(150)	360
Product D	250	300	50	1,500	1,400	(100)	280
Total	760	821	61	4,560	3,977	(583)	1,028

Look at product A – note that sales by volume are slightly below budget. For product B, sales are slightly ahead of budget. But now look at the figures for sales by value.

Sales by value (month six)

	Month			Year to date			Last year
	Budget	*Actual*	*Variance*	*Budget*	*Actual*	*Variance*	*Month*
Product A	3,000	4,998	1,998	18,000	21,998	3,998	3,000
Product B	2,200	1,404	(796)	13,200	9,996	(3,204)	1,750
Product C	4,000	4,400	400	24,000	18,000	(6,000)	1,800
Product D	2,500	3,000	500	15,000	14,000	(1,000)	2,800
Total	£11,700	£13,802	£2,102	£70,200	£63,994	£(6,206)	£9,350

For product A, actual sales revenue has exceeded budgeted sales revenue by nearly £2,000 for the month. This is because the price has been increased from £10 to £17, without apparently a major impact on the sales volume. Product B, however, has had its price cut from £20 to £12. This has had little effect on sales by volume. Whether dropping or increasing the price is likely to have an impact on sales by volume depends on the product's price elasticity (see page 77).

These changes can be illustrated graphically as shown in the chart overleaf for product B. The price variance is shown on the y (vertical) axis and the volume variance is shown on the x (horizontal) axis. The total income, in each case, is the area bounded by the graph. (That is, if you multiply the two sides, it will give the total income.) The budgeted sales price of £20 with sales of 110 would generate £2,200 for the month. The actual sales price of £12 with sales of 117 units generates only £1,404. This gives a negative variance of £796.

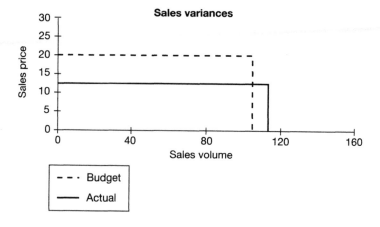

This potentially gives two problems. If your direct costs are constant, say, £8 per unit, then the contribution per unit has dropped from £12 to £4. Although the sales volume has gone up slightly it may not have increased sufficiently to cover the fixed costs attributed to this product, but at least this product is still making a positive contribution. If you sell more than one product, the final variance may disguise substantial variances of the individual products. You must therefore look very carefully at the individual product variances.

> Sales figures are very important – you need to pick up trends quickly. A downturn in sales will require a cut back in expenditure if the trend continues for too long.

You should also look regularly at your order and enquiry position. Do you have enough orders for next month? Do you have enquiries that might quickly be turned into firm orders? If the answer to both of these is no, then you need to be working harder to promote your business.

Materials and labour variances

As with sales variances, analysis of raw material, sub-contract and direct labour costs needs to look both at the cost variance and at the usage variance. One might be favourable, but the other might be unfavourable.

Let's look closer at Katie's product C, which is made entirely of wood. Katie has budgeted for the year to pay £5 per square metre for wood and worked on the assumption that each unit will require 3 square metres allowing for wastage and breakage. Thus each unit, on average, has raw material costs of £15. If she achieves her monthly budget of 100 units she will spend £1,500 on raw materials.

When Katie looks at the actual figures for month six, she finds that the cost has risen to £7 per square metre but her average usage has fallen to 2.5 square metres. The variance per unit is, therefore, £(2.50). The total variance, because the number of doors sold has increased, is £(425). This calculation is shown in the table below.

Product C: Materials usage: Wood

	Budget			Actual			Variance
	Sq m	£	Total	Sq m	£	Total	
per unit	3	5	15	2.5	7	17.50	(2.50)
per total sales	300		1,500	275		1,925	(425)

Note that the extra sales of this product achieved a favourable variance of £400 so even though she has increased her sales by volume by 10 per cent, and reduced material usage by 17 per cent, she has actually made a contribution which is £25 lower than her budget. This can also be illustrated graphically as shown below.

Raw material variances

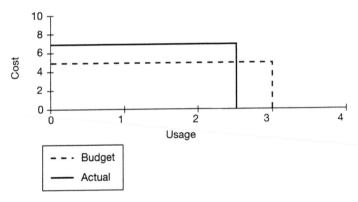

As with the sales variance, the cost variance is shown on the y axis and the usage variance is shown on the x axis. The total cost of materials, per unit, is the area bounded by the graph, that is, the amount resulting from multiplying together the two sides. It is important to understand why the figures are changing. It is quite possible for a favourable movement in raw material cost to be cancelled by increased wastage, for example. This will not show up immediately in the figures extracted from the accounting records, but variance analysis should help to identify which, and this is essential if costs are to be kept under control.

Similar calculations can be employed for wages, labour efficiency and overheads.

Overheads variances

Variances in overheads are easier to monitor. For fixed overheads, any variance is simply caused by spending more or less money. Provided these costs are under control, and provided sales targets are being achieved, problems are unlikely to arise. If, however, margins are low and the targets are not being achieved then contributions may not cover the fixed costs.

Variances of variable overheads are more difficult to track. Some should be watched carefully. If you have a high demand for electrical power, you will have a peak power meter installed and may find yourself on a tariff that changes if you use more power than agreed with your local electricity company. This should, therefore, be monitored in a similar way to raw material usage.

Overheads

	Month			Year to date		
	Budget	Actual	Variance	Budget	Actual	Variance
Production	1,200	1,300	(100)	7,200	5,850	1,350
Administration	200	200	0	1,200	1,200	0
Marketing	300	400	(100)	1,800	1,800	0
Distribution	300	250	50	1,800	1,500	300
Total	2,000	2,150	(150)	12,000	10,350	1,650

It was suggested in Chapter 3 that you group fixed costs together under headings such as marketing, distribution and administration and that you restrict these to a percentage of sales revenue as well as aiming to match your budgeted figures. As with other ratios, these figures can be compared year on year and against competitors. Monthly figures can, of course, be distorted by exceptional items, like a big order or a series of quarterly costs all falling due at the same time. However, these should have been allowed for in the forecast, so should not come as a surprise.

Selling costs

Selling costs include all marketing and advertising costs as well as the cost of any sales people that you employ together with distribution costs, though I have shown marketing costs and distribution costs separately in the example above. Are the marketing costs being contained? Is the effort put into selling reflected in the sales figures? Watching this figure carefully will also provide data to assist in the preparation of demand curves. Is your method of distribution efficient, effective and economical? Is there any scope to reduce the distribution costs?

Production costs

Production costs normally cover all the costs associated with production that are not direct costs. This might include, for example, labour (if not treated as direct labour), premises costs and repairs and maintenance.

Administration costs

Administration costs cover all the office costs and any costs that cannot easily be apportioned to the other headings. Are they being contained? Is there scope for savings? On the other hand, if they are too low, is customer service suffering?

Allocating overheads

While it will undoubtedly help in setting accurate prices, it can be extremely difficult to allocate overhead costs fairly across a number of products. As explained earlier, in the chapter on costing and pricing, you must at the very least ensure that every sale covers the direct costs, that is, that the product or service is making a contribution.

161

Controlling overheads

The big challenge, however is to control overheads, especially once your business starts to grow. Left alone, they will grow even faster and start to eat into profits. It is all too easy to buy another computer, or to upgrade the photocopier, or to take on extra staff, especially if the business is generating cash. But you need continually to consider what this might do to the profit margins.

Regularly review all your overheads in an effort to reduce your cost base.

Don't forget that you may not be able to spend the profit. If you have heavy capital expenditure it is possible to be operating profitably when the cashflow is strongly negative. Similarly, you may have an increasing level of working capital tied up in stock or your customers may be extending the delay before they pay you.

Decor by Diane

You are reviewing the monthly sales figures for Decor by Diane. Diane's original estimate of sales for the month was 20 jobs at an average price, excluding VAT but including paint and other direct costs, of £650. Her actual sales were £13,100.

- Is this sales figure good or bad?

- What variances do you need to look at more closely?

- One job missed the deadline so Diane had to pay overtime of £750 to complete it over a weekend. More paint than expected was consumed during the month, costing a further £200. What do you think about the figures now?

The operating statement

Combining the revenue, direct costs and overhead costs enables you to prepare a monthly operating statement. This records income and expenditure (as does the profit and loss account), not receipt and payments. It may ignore some items such as depreciation or bad debts. It should, however, give a close approximation to the actual profit and loss account.

Each month, you should compare your actual performance with your forecast both for the month and, ideally, for the year to date.

If you have a computerised accounting package, this will be a very simple task. The example below shows budget, actual and variance. Note that it also shows different costs as a percentage of sales price, as suggested in Chapter 4. If you set targets for each of these, they will quickly show up in a report like this.

Selecting the 'budget' option in Sage accounting systems will provide a report like this for you at the touch of a button.

Particularly note the gross profit margin. You will quickly discover the profit margin required to cover all your fixed costs. Newsagents, for example, work on a margin of 16–22 per cent; fashion shops might expect 40–50 per cent; manufacturers might aim for 60–80 per cent depending on the product. If the gross profit margin is falling, it could be a sign of trouble. Has wastage increased? Has the cost increased? Service businesses with no, or very low, direct costs, will have a very high margin and may not find this such a helpful figure to watch. Instead, they might find it helpful to monitor actual sales and compare the figure with the monthly break-even point.

Operating statement (month six)

	Month Budget		Month Actual		Month Variance	Year to date Budget		Year to date Actual		Year to date Variance
Sales revenue	4,000	100%	4,400	100%	400	24,000	100%	18,000	100%	(6,000)
less: direct costs										
Materials	1,500	38%	1,925	44%	(425)	9,000	38%	7,000	39%	2,000
Sub-contract		0%		0%	0		0%		0%	0
Total direct	1,500	38%	1,925	44%	(425)	9,000	38%	7,000	39%	2,000
Gross profit	2,500	63%	2,475	56%	(25)	15,000	63%	11,000	61%	(4,000)
less: overheads										
Production	1,200	30%	1,300	30%	(100)	7,200	30%	5,850	33%	1,350
Administration	200	5%	200	5%	0	1,200	5%	1,200	7%	0
Marketing	300	8%	400	9%	(100)	1,800	8%	1,800	10%	0
Distribution	300	8%	250	6%	50	1,800	8%	1,500	8%	300
Total overheads	2,000	50%	2,150	49%	(150)	12,000	50%	10,350	58%	1,650
Net operating profit	500	13%	325	7%	(175)	3,000	13%	650	4%	(2,350)

Contribution by product line

An alternative to the operating statement is to look at contribution by product, though many people prefer the former format with or without the overhead analysis. Looking at contribution by product will help you to assess whether individual products are profitable. In order to calculate contribution accurately, all the variable costs need to be deducted though, in practice, defining variable costs is a good deal more difficult than it first appears. The effort of allocating overhead costs by product will probably involve too much administration for a small firm.

EXAMPLE

William's Widgets

William's only variable costs are material costs, so it is very easy to calculate the contribution, which you should note is the same as the gross profit figure in the operating statement.

164

	Budget (year to date)					Actual (year to date)				
	Sales revenue	Variable materials	Variable labour	Variable other	Contrib.	Sales revenue	Variable materials	Variable labour	Variable other	Contrib.
Product A	18,000	7,200			10,800	22,000	8,800			13,200
Product B	13,000	4,300			8,700	10,000	4,250			5,750
Product C	13,000	4,300			8,700	9,000	3,950			5,050
Product D	15,000	5,000			10,000	14,000	6,000			8,000
	59,000	20,800	0	0	38,200	55,000	23,000	0	0	32,000

EXAMPLE

Gabriel's Glazing

Now look at the next figures which show an analysis of two services offered by Gabriel's Glazing. This business buys in materials for assembly and installation, and for installation only.

	Budget (year to date)					Actual (year to date)				
	Sales revenue	Variable materials	Variable labour	Variable other	Contrib.	Sales revenue	Variable materials	Variable labour	Variable other	Contrib.
Assembly & installation	200,000	80,000	40,000	6,000	74,000	220,000	90,000	35,000	5,000	90,000
Installation only	100,000	10,000	20,000	3,000	67,000	50,000	5,000	10,000	3,500	31,500
	300,000	90,000	60,000	9,000	141,000	270,000	95,000	45,000	8,500	121,500

As explained earlier, the contribution goes first towards covering the overhead costs and then towards profit. Every product or service must therefore make a positive contribution or else it should be discontinued, unless there has been a positive decision to sell as a loss-leader.

The cash flow statement

The operating statement shows the net trading profit but does not give any indication of the liquidity of the business. It is therefore worthwhile also preparing a monthly cash flow statement as shown below. If, at the beginning of each year, you prepare a cash flow forecast with columns for forecast and actual for each month, preparing this statement will be relatively easy. The cash flow statement reflects when money is received or paid out and includes items such as drawings, VAT or tax, which are not regarded as trading expenses. The cash flow statement is often the easiest financial statement to produce, because all the figures should be readily available from the cash book.

Managing the net cash flow can be more important in the short term than managing the net profit, because it allows for the timing of receipts and payments as well as for the amounts.

	Month			Year to date		
	Budget	Actual	Variance	Budget	Actual	Variance
Receipts						
Sales – cash	0	0	0	0	0	0
Sales – credit	9,900	3,800	(6,100)	59,000	47,800	(11,200)
VAT	1,733	665	(1,068)	10,325	8,365	(1,960)
Sales of assets	0	0	0	0	0	0
Other receipts	0	0	0	0	0	0
Total	11,633	4,465	(7,168)	69,325	56,105	(13,160)
Payments						
Purchases – cash	0	0	0	0	0	0
Purchases – credit	3,800	3,150	650	20,800	21,500	(700)
Wages	2,000	2,000	0	12,000	11,500	500
Overheads	2,850	2,800	50	25,000	20,300	4,700
Capital	2,000	2,000	0	5,000	2,000	3,000
VAT	1,514	1,392	122	8,890	7,665	1,225
Loan repayments	500	500	0	3,000	3,000	0
Drawings	1,000	1,000	0	6,000	6,000	0
Other	0	0	0	0	0	0
Total	13,664	12,842	822	80,690	71,965	8,725
Net cashflow	(2,031)	(8,377)	(6,346)	(11,365)	(15,860)	(4,435)
Balance at start						
Cash	3,492	5,373		13,000	13,000	
Overdraft						
Balance at end						
Cash	1,461			1,635		
Overdraft		(3,004)			(2,800)	

Aged debtors

Some form of aged debtors report will be produced by most computer systems. Usually the debt will be listed for each customer. This is one of the most useful reports available and is often the prime reason for installing a computerised accounting system.

	Current month	30 days	60 days	90 days	over 90 days	Total	
This month	8,000	4,800	1,200	100	0	14,100	
Last month	9,000	3,400	900			13,300	

Analysis of debtors

Debtors	Current month	30 days	60 days	90 days	over 90 days	Total	Credit limit
J Bloggs		2,800				2,800	3,000
D Smith	500		200	100		800	1,000
Crumbs Ltd	5,000	2,000				7,000	10,000
Ballyhoo	2,500		1,000			3,500	5,000
						0	
						0	
	8,000	4,800	1,200	100	0	14,100	

Even if you do not have a computer, you should easily be able to derive a list of aged debtors from your sales ledger. Calculate the average debt collection period. Has it got better – or worse? Are your customers paying promptly? Clearly, a reduction in the collection period will improve your cash flow.

Aged creditors

Normally people are more concerned with getting their money in than paying out on time. However, payment outside of the terms of credit can lead to bad feeling and disruption of supplies. This report can serve as a check on the work of the accounts payable department to ensure that payments are being made within a reasonable period but not too early! An extension in the credit period taken will obviously improve your cash flow, but you need to beware of upsetting your suppliers. Conversely a reduction in the credit period will have a detrimental effect on your cash flow.

	Current month	30 days	60 days	90 days	over 90 days	Total	
This month	5,000	7,000	500		0	12,500	
Last month	4,000	3,000	2,000			9,000	

Top ten creditors

Creditors	Current month	30 days	60 days	90 days	over 90 days	Total	Credit limit
Richard Harvey	1,000	1,500				2,500	3,000
Tinker & Wood Ltd		500	500			1,000	1,000
Vehicle Supplies Ltd		2,000				2,000	10,000
Matsupplies	4,000	3,000				7,000	5,000
						0	
						0	
	5,000	7,000	500	0	0	12,500	

As with the debtors, you should review your payment period regularly. You will wish to ensure that you maximise the period of borrowing from your suppliers, because that is cheaper than borrowing from the bank, whilst staying within your agreed terms of trade.

Stock

It is very easy to tie up too much working capital in maintaining high stock levels, so monitor the total amount of stock that you are carrying and aim to keep it as low as possible, commensurate with keeping sufficient raw materials to keep production going and sufficient finished goods to satisfy your customers. As with sales and direct costs, stock should be monitored on an individual product basis.

Stock	Month		Year to date	
	Budget	Actual	Budget	Actual
Start of period	2,000	1,900	2,000	2,000
Purchases	1,500	3,375	9,000	8,350
Stock used	1,500	1,925	9,000	7,000
End of period	2,000	3,350	2,000	3,350
Average	2,000	2,625	2,000	2,675

Do you know what the stock turnover ratio should be for your business? If not, find out.

Capital expenditure report

This report will prove most useful if there is a continuing programme of building works or major capital expenditure on equipment. Building projects are almost invariably late and overspent. A report such as this, prepared monthly or quarterly, at least alerts management on a regular basis to potential problems. The example, taken from Sage Financial Controller, shows capital expenditure for Katie's Kitchens.

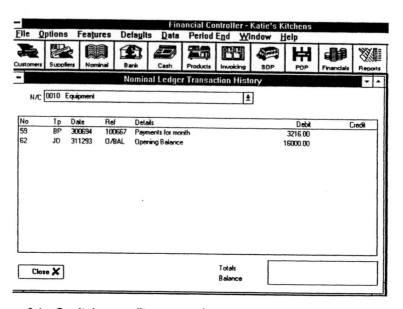

Figure 9.1　Capital expenditure record

For most small businesses this will probably be unnecessary, though do not forget to include all capital expenditure in your cash flow.

Labour turnover report

If your business employs large numbers of staff it makes sense to look at labour turnover and at rates of sickness and absence. A high labour turnover figure can be significant because it may indicate dissatisfaction with working conditions or management. High labour turnover can be expensive in retraining staff.

The balance sheet

Once the figures are available for the analysis described above, you are in a position to prepare the balance sheet. Some items may fluctuate considerably from month to month. Others, for example the fixed assets, will show little change. If changes in stock and work in progress are slow, it may be preferable to check the actual levels less frequently, say, quarterly or annually. You should, however, be able to calculate a value for stock and work in progress.

Unless you have computerised your book-keeping, you may decide to prepare this report less frequently than monthly. In that case, you must prepare an alternative monthly report which at least shows the cash available, the total debtors and the total creditors. These three figures enable you to calculate the quick ratio.

	Last month	Current month	Change %
Fixed assets			
Land & buildings			
Plant & machinery	5,000	5,000	0%
Fixtures etc.	3,500	3,500	0%
Motor vehicles	2,000	4,000	100%
Total fixed assets	10,500	12,500	19%
Current assets			
Stock, (S)	1,900	3,350	76%
Work in progress, (S)	1,800	1,229	-32%
Finished goods, (S)	1,500	6,700	347%
Debtors	13,300	14,100	6%
Bank			
Cash	1,430		
Total current assets, (A)	19,930	25,379	27%
Current liabilities			
Creditors	9,000	12,500	39%
Overdraft		2,900	
Loans	4,500	4,000	-11%
Tax			
Total current liabilities, (L)	13,500	19,400	44%
Net current assets	6,430	5,980	-7%
Total net assets	16,930	18,480	9%
Represented by:			
Owners' capital	8,000	8,000	0%
Reserves	8,930	10,480	17%
Total capital employed	16,930	18,480	9%

$$Current\ ratio = A/L = \frac{25{,}379}{19{,}400} = 1.31$$

$$Quick\ ratio = (A{-}S)/L = \frac{14{,}100}{19{,}400} = 0.73$$

Comparing the current ratio (1.3) in the example with the target (at least 1.5) suggests that the business is somewhat exposed. The quick ratio, at 0.7, is just about on the bottom limit of acceptability. However, if the element of the bank loan repayable in more than one year is omitted, the current ratio improves to 1.4. If all the bank loan is omitted, since the repayment terms are fixed, the current ratio improves further to 1.65 and the quick ratio to 0.9.

Review the figures with your staff

170   It was suggested earlier that the relevant staff should be involved in drawing up the budget for your business and that they should be encouraged to feel responsible for keeping costs under control. If they are to do that effectively they should get copies of the figures as soon as they are available. In addition, however, you should have regular financial review meetings, particularly for staff with financial responsibilities.

> You should ensure that you meet with your staff regularly to review the variances together to decide what action, if any, needs to be taken and, crucially, to decide who should be taking that action.

It is equally important, if everything is on target, to praise staff for achieving the plan. It is a frequent complaint that managers are quick to criticise but never give praise, so seize the opportunities when they present themselves.

Use of spreadsheets

A spreadsheet package is particularly useful, in preparing cash flow forecasts together with the associated profit and loss account and balance sheet. Once budgets have been set and the forecasts prepared, it is possible to look at effects of changes in sales or costs (i.e. perform a sensitivity analysis). If you don't think your budget is completely realistic, it is extremely easy to change a few of the figures.

There is a wide range of spreadsheet packages available that can speed up the preparation of financial forecasts and give considerable help in the analysis of actual results giving speedy comparisons with budgets. Well-known packages include Lotus 1–2–3 and Microsoft Excel. In addition to calculating figures rapidly, a good spreadsheet will also enable you to produce graphs quickly and accurately. Many of the spreadsheets and all of the graphical illustrations in this book were prepared using Excel. Once set up, you only need to enter new data each month. It is extremely easy, however, to get so carried away that you produce far more information than you require. Remember the earlier point about concentrating on just a few key variables. Then use the computer facilities to assist in their preparation. Hard work is still required to prepare the figures initially. Do not fall into the mistake of assuming they must be correct because the computer says so.

Look at the next example which shows the cash flow forecast for Catherine's Chairs, this time with columns for actuals, budgets and variances, set up using Microsoft Excel.

171

			A17		Drawings			
	A	B	C	D
1	Catherine's Chairs: Cashflow statement			
2		Total to date	Budget to date	Variance
3	Sales by value	37,200	40,000	(2,800)
4	Receipts			
5	Cash	12,400	14,000	(1,600)
6	Debtors	14,400	16,000	(1,600)
7	VAT	4,690	5,250	(560)
8	Loans	5,000	5,000	0
9	Total	36,490	40,250	(3,760)
10	Payments			
11	Trade creditors	15,000	16,000	1,000
12	Overheads	6,400	6,000	(400)
13	Equipment	0	1,000	1,000
14	Wages	4,000	4,000	0
15	Loan repayments	1,600	1,600	0
16	Interest	200	200	0
17	Drawings	4,000	4,500	500
18	VAT	3,745	4,025	280
19	VAT to C&E	1,050	1,350	300
20	Total	35,995	38,675	2,680

Figure 9.2   Cash flow statement

Spreadsheet packages really come into their own turning figures into graphs. Look at the next figure, for example, which shows monthly sales together with a three-month and a six-month moving average. Moving averages, regression analysis, correlation and other functions, all easily available at the touch of one or two keys, will assist in sales forecasting, in looking at the effect of advertising on sales and, as suggested earlier, in monitoring actual sales against target sales.

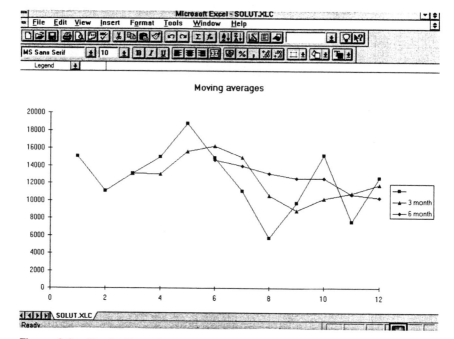

Figure 9.3   Illustration of computer graphics

Conclusion and checklist

If you are going to monitor and control your business effectively you must:

- Prepare a budget which is realistic and achievable, though probably at least a little challenging also; and
- Ensure that you monitor performance regularly, at least monthly, against that budget.

You may feel that this is time-consuming and unnecessary, but it is absolutely essential if you are to remain in complete control of your business. The important areas to watch are:

- Sales variances
  - sales price variances
  - sales volume variances
- Material variances
  - material cost variances
  - material usage variances
- Labour variances
  - activity variances
  - wages variances
- Overheads variances
- Operating statement
- Cashflow statement
- Aged debtors
- Aged creditors
- Stock position.

Are all your products making a positive contribution? Do all the contributions together cover your fixed costs? Are you on target? Is the money coming in or are the aged debtors getting too large? Are you still profitable? Are you still liquid? Are you still solvent?

You may find that you do not need to monitor all of these figures – but you should quickly find out which are the crucial ones for your business. Use the facilities of a computerised accounting package and a spreadsheet package. Once properly set up, they will speed up considerably the process of extracting the appropriate and relevant information. You need to use that information to retain effective control of the business and, if necessary, to see where it may be necessary to take corrective action.

173

10

Using the figures

> Once you have gained a picture of the operating position of your business, you need to use the figures to assess your performance and, where necessary, to take corrective action.

We have now almost come full circle round the Plan Do Check Act cycle introduced in Chapter 2. We have looked at the requirements for effective data recording and, particularly, effective book-keeping. We have looked at techniques such as ratio analysis and variance analysis in order to compare your performance with your targets.

Among smaller businesses, many fail to introduce a proper financial control system though increasingly they are being encouraged to put in place such a system. Sadly, however, too many of those then fail to use the figures to keep control of their business. Hopefully, by the time you have read this far, you will not only appreciate the importance of using the figures but also will have already got a feel for the most important figures to monitor. As you look at financial statements more frequently you will find that understanding the figures becomes considerably easier. Computerised accounting packages make it very easy to prepare the figures, though care does have to be taken to avoid mistakes creeping in and to spot mistakes if they do.

The aim of this last chapter is to summarise the key areas where you will need to concentrate your attention.

Sales and costs

Whilst it is essential to set targets for profitability (such as net profit margin and return on capital employed) and to monitor progress towards achieving those targets, it may not be immediately clear what needs to be done to get back on track if there is a variance. If, as suggested in Chapter 4, you work down the ratio tree, translating the profitability targets into targets for sales and for different costs as percentages of sales, then it will be fairly obvious what needs to be done to keep the business on target or to get back on target if the businss should stray. Review your order book regularly. Three key figures to monitor are

- value of orders placed in a given period;
- value of production completed; and,
- sales invoiced.

Do you have enough orders of sufficient size for your next trading period? Is your level of gross profit high enough ? If the answer to either of these questions is no, you need to market your business to win some extra business. If that is unsuccessful, you need to look at whether you can cut the costs incurred by the business until orders pick up again. Use the ratios of costs to sales. If there are substantial differences in sales or costs, and if it appears that you will not be able to take action which gets you back on target, then you will need to prepare a revised budget and, in particular, identify whether you will still be making a profit and whether you will have sufficient working capital to cope with your revised forecast.

It is also essential to act quickly if debtors and creditors should stray too far from target, as this will affect the business's liquidity and, probably, its overdraft.

175

Debtors

If your business is sending out sales invoices, then a tight grip must be kept to ensure the debtors' position is both known and acceptable. Your sales ledger clearly shows all your outstanding sales invoices. Review them regularly, preferably on a weekly basis but at the very least on a monthly basis. If any customer is slow in paying you, chase them hard. There is no hard and fast rule about the length of credit that you can give customers, but 30 or 60 days is normal in many business sectors. In some it is considerably longer. If the level of debtors rises this could be because your sales are increasing or because your debtors are taking longer to pay. Ensure that you define in your terms of trade how quickly you expect debtors to pay and then try to ensure that they stick to it. Much invoicing is still left until the end of the month with consequent disastrous results on cash flow.

Issue all sales invoices as soon as possible after the work is done; the sooner they are issued the sooner, in general, they will be paid and your business will receive the money.

This can then be used to pay for more goods or reduce your overdraft, thus saving bank interest. The timing of invoices can have a substantial effect on cash flow. No matter what your stated credit terms, most businesses tend to pay at the end of the month following invoice date. It makes sense therefore, if possible, to raise and date invoices at the end of a month rather than at the start of the next month. If a customer is paying net monthly, an invoice dated 31 March would be paid on 30 April whereas a 1 April invoice would not be paid until 31 May. If you are not paid within your agreed collection period, issue a statement. Some businesses get into the habit of never paying until a statement arrives. If you do not regularly send out statements, mark on your original invoice that statements will not be issued.

If you need the money urgently ring your customer and politely but firmly enquire when you will receive what is owed to you. Ring more than once if necessary. Be careful about being fobbed off with excuses, for example: 'The director is away and we can't get the cheque signed', or, 'It's in the post'. Note these and if it doesn't come within two days, ring again.

If, after several weeks the money is not forthcoming, and the debt is large enough, legal action may be necessary. This is the last resort so keep pursuing the customer with phone calls first. In many circumstances, a series of reminder letters, each worded more strongly than the last, is enough to ensure payment before potential legal action. Legal action is expensive and takes up valuable time, though smaller claims can be dealt with relatively quickly and cheaply through the Small Claims procedure in the County Court. One trick adopted by some small business people, when owed money by large customers, is simply to sit in their reception area or, better still, outside their front door with a large placard and wait until the cheque is produced.

Credit references

If large orders from unknown customers are placed with you, it may make sense to obtain a credit reference. Ask for trade references and also for a bank reference. Consult a credit reference agency; Dun and Bradstreet is the most well known, but there may be a smaller one locally. Companies such as Infolink and Infotech offer computerised on-line facilities for obtaining instant credit references. There is obviously a cost associated with any credit check but this could certainly outweigh the potential cost of bad debt, especially in the case of a large contract. In addition, you may choose not to give too high a level of credit until your customers have built up a good record of paying you promptly.

Creditors

Keeping control of the money you owe others can be done in a similar fashion to the way you control money owed to you. Review all the bills you have to pay at least monthly. Do not upset your suppliers by delaying payment for too long, otherwise they may withdraw your credit facilities. It takes time to build up a good track record with suppliers, but when you do, working on credit becomes easier. To gain the most benefit, however, you need to take the maximum amount of credit possible without abusing the terms agreed with your suppliers.

As with debtors, the timing of purchases can have a substantial effect on cash flow. If your suppliers' terms are payable by the end of the month following invoice date then it is better to have an invoice dated, say 1 May than one dated 30 April. Some companies deliver goods in the last week before a month end, even if the order was placed for the following week! If your stock levels allow, you should try not to place orders for the last week of a month, and if your supplier delivers early you should not accept the goods until your required delivery date.

177

You need to take particular care to ensure your PAYE and VAT payments are made on time, otherwise you could incur substantial penalties.

There has been much discussion in the press about how to encourage or force businesses to pay their suppliers more quickly, particularly where the suppliers are small businesses. The Government intends to introduce legislation during 1995 to compel public limited companies and their subsidiaries to disclose in their annual report their policy on payment. It is good practice, however, for all businesses to have a payments policy and to monitor their average payment period to ensure that they comply with the policy.

If you are controlling your debtors and creditors carefully then you will also be controlling the business's working capital carefully. There are two possible scenarios. In one, you need an overdraft to cover costs until the debtors pay; in the other you have money in the bank. Many businesses hover around a zero balance sometimes needing an overdraft and sometimes being in credit. If you find yourself, however, with a substantial overdraft or with a substantial credit balance you might wish to do something about it, such as investing the surplus cash or raising term loans.

Cash management

Do you have large sums of money simply sitting in a current account? Is it likely to be there for long? If you do have substantial cash balances, make it work for you. All the banks have special arrangements for putting large sums on deposit – frequently directly on the sterling money market. Interest rates are often within a couple of percentage points of the bank base rate. In general, the longer the period for which you are prepared to tie up your money, the better the rate of interest that can be obtained. Clearly, it makes sense not to become too illiquid by tying up all your spare cash for too long. If you are likely to need some or all of your cash quickly, do not put it into long-term investments. Most banks can make arrangements to transfer excess bank balances to a deposit or investment account automatically and vice versa. This can increase investment income while keeping cash available to use.

You could also, of course, look at whether you should be investing some or all of your cash back into the business. Should you be upgrading equipment? Are there opportunities for expansion? Are there new business opportunities? Remember the tips in the chapter on capital appraisal, however. How do you get the best return on that money right now? Once again, it might be prudent not to invest all of it in this way but to keep at least some for expanded working capital requirements.

If sales increase, debtors will also rise. But, unless you can find the increased working capital requirement from retained earnings or by increasing the level of creditors, you will need to increase your overdraft facility. Keep your bank informed well in advance. If they won't help then you may find yourself in the position where you have to turn down extra work – or negotiate a suitable deposit or agree staged payments. As suggested in Chapter 7, you may wish to look at factoring or invoice discounting to speed up the receipt of the money you are owed, though there is a cost associated with both of these.

> If you have a 'hard-core' overdraft, it would make sense to convert into a term loan repayable over, say, three or five years or even longer. Loans have the advantage that they cannot be recalled at will, unlike overdrafts and it may be possible to negotiate a fixed rate of interest on a loan.

Overdrafts usually require to be renewed at least once each year incurring bank charges and always have a variable rate of interest. The banks all have penal rates of interest for unauthorised overdrafts, so you need to take particular care not to exceed your facility.

Cash management also requires a careful look at your cash flow forecast for the previous, the current and the following months. At the end of each month, use the column headed 'actual' on your cash flow forecast to fill in your actual performance. Does this indicate a need to take corrective action? Are there implications for future cash flow? Can you time payments after your receipts? Will you remain within your overdraft facility? Do you need to arrange extra provision? Remember that if you do foresee difficulties it is better to advise your bankers before the problems arise rather than burying your head in the sand and perhaps waiting for the banks to contact you. If you take positive action in this way it will demonstrate to the bank that you are actually in control, and may favourably affect their options. Similarly the banks have business advisers who may be able to assist you. It is obviously better to obtain assistance as a prevention rather than a cure.

Stock control

Do not allow your stock levels to grow too large and watch for dead stock. If you have too much stock, you will be taking up too much storage space. Can you reduce it and use the space more productively? If your current ratio is static and your quick ratio is falling, you may have a problem with stock. Is this because sales are falling? Or are you buying too much raw materials? Or is your work in progress too high? If you do have obsolete stock or stock movement problems, you either need to write it off or turn it into cash as quickly as possible. Possible cut-off problems include accepting deliveries just before the end of the month or not invoicing until the beginning of the next month.

179

Improving capital efficiency

The only ways in which you can make your capital work harder is either by increasing the asset turn – that is, achieving a high level of sales with no additional capital – or by increasing the gearing – increasing the use of borrowed funds as a proportion of capital employed. If you have expensive capital equipment, are you maximising its output? You do not want expensive equipment lying idle since it doesn't generate income, but it still depreciates. If there is demand for your products, can you introduce a system of shift working? Can you sell spare capacity to another business? Would you be better off selling the machine (or not buying it in the first place) and sub-contracting the operation for which the machine is used?

Paying creditors as late as possible, but within agreed terms of trade, will keep down the level of working capital required and, thus, the total assets. This requires tight control.

Improving staff efficiency

Efficiency is usually a measure of a volume of activity. Do you believe that your staff are working as efficiently and effectively as possible? Are there ways in which you can improve that efficiency? Possible indicators of problems amongst staff are high labour turnover ratios and high levels of sickness absence. One way is to encourage more competition between staff, perhaps with performance bonuses and prizes. There is always the danger, however, of sabotage. What you require is to encourage the development of a team spirit, so that everyone pulls together for the good of the business. Perhaps a performance bonus based on total results might be appropriate. In this case, however, watch out for those not pulling their weight. While they might be carried by the other staff initially, they will quickly cause resentment.

EXAMPLE

Fulprint

Bob Scrase, who runs Fulprint, a printing business based in York, uses the concept of added value to assist his sales reps to maximise profit for the business. As he notes, his sales reps can always make a sale by dropping the price. There is a danger, however, that the gross profit margin falls too low to cover the overheads. To combat this, the sales reps' commission is now governed by their added value performance, rather than by their total sales performance.

Although the added value calculation was easy for the computer, it was not so easy for the sales reps to understand! So Fulprint introduced a modification, such that all jobs are categorised into added value bands. The target added value is 65 per cent of sales price. For each 5 per cent achieved over this target, the sales rep receives additional commission of 2 per cent of sales price, giving a likely maximum of 8 per cent on top of the normal commission of 5 per cent of sales price.

Would different machines improve efficiency? Do you regularly ask your staff for their suggestions? Do they see their work merely as 'a job' or something they want to do? Take an interest in career development. Provide training and development opportunities. Encourage further training, even if it is not directly related to their work. Undertake regular appraisals. Praise staff when they do well. This is at least as important, and maybe more so, than criticising poor performance, and can even be as effective as a wage increase.

Lastly, keep all your staff well informed about the business's objectives, its performance and its progress. Do not spend all your time sitting behind a desk in an office with the door closed. Talk regularly to all your staff. Let them see that you are committed and they will try harder also. Your objective should be to build morale and maintain a happy workforce.

Conclusion and checklist

Deriving the performance figures for a business is relatively straight-forward. It is essential to understand the figures and to use those figures for effective control. Are you controlling the finances of your business effectively? Choose a set of targets which are appropriate for your business. IBM, for example, monitors the performance of its subsidiaries through seven measures. Four are financial: revenue growth, profit, return on assets and cash flow. The other three, echoing the approach of Jack Welch of the US company, General Electric, are customer satisfaction, quality and staff morale. Which measures will you use? You might like to consider the following questions:

- Does the business set targets? In particular, do you set targets for sales and profitability? Do you have an effective management information system? Do you receive, or can you extract, appropriate information as required?
- Does the business have an effective sales control system? Do you constantly review your order position and look at ways of improving the marketing of the business? Do you review debtors regularly and chase them for prompt payment?
- Does the business control stock effectively? Do you regularly review material ordering procedures and aim for just-in-time stock control?
- Does the business control the production system effectively, limiting levels of work in progress? Do you limit the build up of finished goods?
- Does the business control effectively the quality of its product or service?
- Does the business have effective expense control procedures? Do you regularly explore ways to reduce costs. Do you review creditors regularly and make payments within the agreed terms?
- Does the business manage its cash position effectively? Do you know the level of cash in the bank right now? Do you take action early when an increase in overdraft will be required? Do you invest spare cash effectively?
- Does the business monitor its performance? Do you look regularly at the actual performance and compare it with the forecast? Do you take corrective action if the variances are not favourable?
- Has the business computerised its accounting and management

181

information systems? If not, it may be worth considering whether that would improve the effectiveness of your control.

Remember always that, for most businesses, profit is the relatively small difference between two large numbers – price and cost. If you can keep your prices high and your costs low, then you will make a profit – which can be shared amongst the owners and reinvested to assist the business to survive and prosper.

Finally, remember that cash, and control of cash, is of primary importance. It is the lifeblood of all businesses. Without sufficient cash available, any business will fail.

Glossary

■

Absorption costing A method of costing that does not distinguish between fixed and variable costs in the calculation of the total cost; the total costs are simply divided by the total number of units produced.

Added value The value that you add to a product or service. The price of your product or service equals the cost of the raw materials bought in plus the value that you add. Added value is equal to the overhead costs attributed to the particular product plus your profit. The major element of value added is the contribution by you and your colleagues.

Appropriation account The part of the profit and loss account which explains how the profit has been divided or appropriated.

Assets Goods, resources and property belonging to the business.

Balance sheet A statement showing the assets and liabilities of a business at any particular moment in time.

Breakeven point The breakeven point is the point at which the income from sales exactly equals all the costs of the business.

Capital The finance supplied by the proprietors of a business in order to acquire the resources (assets) with which to operate.

Competitive position The standing of a business in relation to its competitors, on aspects such as price, reputation, quality, etc.

Contribution The amount contributed by a sale is the income generated by that sale less the direct cost of producing that product.

Cost leadership A marketing strategy in which the business aims to sell its products or services at a price which is lower than any of its competitors. Compaq, for example, is currently aiming to sell its computers more cheaply than any other manufacturer and is also aiming to have sufficient margin to reduce its prices if it perceives that others are attempting to beat it on price.

Cost of sales The costs which are clearly attributable to a product. This includes raw material costs, sub-contract costs and direct labour.

Creditor One to whom money is owed for goods, cash, services, etc.

Current assets Assets in a cash or near cash state (e.g. cash, debtors, stock).

Debt Money which has been borrowed to finance the business. Debt might be in the form of an overdraft, a term loan or a debenture.

Debtors One who owes money for goods, cash or services supplied.

Depreciation The amount charged to the profit and loss account each year to represent the wear and tear of machinery, equipment or industrial buildings.

Differentiation A marketing strategy in which the business aims to demonstrate that its products or services are different to those of its competitors. Usually, the approach is to provide greater benefit to customers and to seek a higher price in return.

Direct Cost A cost which is directly attributable to a product or service, such as raw materials, sub-contract work or direct labour. The direct cost will be the same for each unit, but will clearly vary with the total number of units.

Direct labour The (cost of) labour directly attributed to the manufacture of a product. This term is typically used in larger businesses where many people are employed in the manufacturing process. In the past, there was more likelihood of such people being hired and fired at will depending on the order level of the business.

Dividend A payment made from profit after tax to the owners of a business.

Drawings If you are self-employed as a sole trader or partner you will draw money from the business at regular intervals. Known as drawings, this is an advance against (net) profit. Remember that you are taxed on all the profit, which includes your drawings.

Efficiency ratios These are a measure of the efficiency of the business, for example, in collecting debts, in paying creditors, in keeping stock to a minimum, etc.

Equity The equity in a business is the (shareholders') capital introduced by the owners, together with any retained earnings.

Expenses A general term which can mean all the costs of a business, but normally used to signify overhead expenses (as opposed to direct costs).

Fixed asset An asset which has a life of longer than one year such as land, buildings, furniture, machinery, etc.

Fixed costs Costs which, generally speaking, are fixed for the business for a reasonable length of time, and not dependent on the number of units produced. These include, for example, rent, rates, salaries, etc.

Focus A marketing strategy in which the business aims for a focused approach on a particular niche market. Since this strategy is unlikey to eliminate competition completely it is usually also necessary to decide on whether to adopt a cost leadership position or a differentiated position within the niche.

Gearing A measure of debt as a proportion of total finance (i.e. ratio of debt/debt plus equity).

Gross profit Normally regarded as the sales income less the direct costs. For many small businesses this will be the same as the contribution.

Industry attractiveness The extent to which a particular segment of a market provides opportunity to make profits, determined by issues such as number of competitors, margins and customer demand.

Interest cover A measure of the ease with which a business can meet its interest requirements. The interest cover is the net profit before interest and tax divided by the interest payable for the same period. Lenders tend to look at this figure!

Invariable costs Costs which do not vary with the number of units produced.

Leverage The ratio of total finance to equity (i.e. ratio of debt plus equity/equity). This term is more commonly used in the US.

Liabilities The combined debts owed by a firm, company, etc.

Liquidity A measure of the working capital or cash available to a business to enable it to meet its liabilities as they fall due. Liquidity ratios include the current ratio and the quick ratio (also known as the 'acid test'). Note that a business can be profitable and still run out of money if it holds too much stock or allows customer credit periods which are too generous.

Margin of safety The margin of safety describes the point above breakeven at which the business is operating. The greater the margin of safety the less sensitive the business will be to falls in sales or increases in costs.

Marginal costing Marginal cost is the extra cost of producing one extra unit. Marginal costing compares the marginal revenue of selling the extra unit with the marginal cost.

Mission statement A statement outlining the purpose of the business; it may also include a description of the vision.

Net profit The actual profit made by the business after the deduction of all expenses. Remember that if you are self-employed, your drawings are not regarded as an expense, whereas wages for your staff, and you if you are director of a company, are expenses. Tax is not regarded as an expense.

Net worth Total assets less total liabilities. Equivalent term to 'net assets'. Equal to shareholders' capital plus retained earnings.

Opportunity cost The income foregone by choosing not to pursue a particular opportunity.

Overtrading The situation that occurs when a business is selling more products or services than its working capital facilities can cope with.

Price elasticity A measure of how sensitive demand for a product or service is to changes in price.

Profit and loss account   A summary of all the income and expenditure for the accounting period.

Profitability   A series of measures which show how profitable a business is. These include gross profit and net profit. Probably the best measure is 'profit before interest and tax', i.e. the sales income less all the direct costs and all the overhead costs except interest. The profit margin is PBIT/sales.

Purpose   Explanation of 'the business that we are in' which guides the activities of the business and defines the key customers.

Reserves   Profits retained within the business.

Revenue   The income generated by the business for a specific period.

Solvency   A measure of a business's ability to pay its bills as they fall due. If it cannot, then it is insolvent.

Standard cost   The total cost of direct labour, direct costs and a suitable proportion of the variable overhead costs incurred in the production process – used to establish how much it will cost to make what is being sold.

Stock   Goods held for sale in the ordinary course of business.

Strategic objectives   The objectives that have been identified as necessary if the vision is to be realised.

Strategy   The plan which will enable the business to develop from where it is now to achieve the vision.

Turnover   Net sales, income that is, total sales less allowances.

Variable costs   Costs which vary with the level of production. These clearly include direct costs such as raw materials. However, other costs, such as power consumption, may also vary with the level of production. These need to be allocated in some way so that the price of the product relates to the labour and resources consumed in its production.

Variance   The difference between budgeted figures and actual figures. Remember that a variance may be a combination of a cost variance and a volume variance, so take care to understand the implications. If a variance is too high, then corrective action will have to be taken to bring the business back on course.

Vision   Where the business is going – statement of desired competitive position outlining challenging but achievable goals with defined timescales.

Zero based forecasting   Forecasting which starts from a zero base rather than on the previous year's actuals.

Further reading

■

The following books may be of interest to those who wish to explore finance and business planning in more depth.

Bull, R J, *Accounting in Business*, Butterworths, 1980.
Irwin, D, *Planning to Succeed in Business*, Pitman Publishing, 1995.
Maitland, I, *Budgeting for Non-financial Managers*, IM/Pitman Publishing, 1995.
Pike, R and Dobbins, R, *Investment Decision and Financial Strategy*, Philip Allan, 1986.
Rice, A, *Accounts Demystified*, IM/Pitman Publishing, 1995.
Walsh, C, *Key Management Ratios*, FT/Pitman Publishing, 1993.

Answers to exercises

■

Chapter 3

Katie's Kitchens: Profit and loss

Profit & Loss Account for year ending 31 December:

	1994		1993	
Sales	1,100,000		750,000	
less: Direct Costs	550,000		375,000	
Gross profit		550,000		375,000
Overheads	370,000		280,000	
Net profit		180,000		95,000
Interest		25,000		24,000
Taxation		38,750		17,750
Dividends		15,000		
Retained		101,250		53,250

The net profit margin in 1994 was 16 per cent. (N.B.: figures for 1993 are given for use in later exercises).

Katie's Kitchens: Balance Sheet

Balance Sheet at 31 December:

	1994		1993	
Fixed Assets				
Equipment	120,000		80,000	
Depreciation	35,000		24,000	
		85,000		56,000
Current assets				
Stock	45,000		25,000	
Debtors	180,000		150,000	
Cash at bank	73,000		35,000	
		298,000		210,000
Current Liabilities				
Loans	30,000		30,000	
Creditors	64,750		50,000	
VAT	20,000		25,000	
Dividends	15,000		0	
Tax	38,750		17,750	
		168,500		122,750
Net current assets		129,500		87,250
Total assets – current liabilities		214,500		143,250
Creditors: amount after 1 year		15,000		45,000

Net assets	199,500	98,250
Represented by:		
Shareholders' capital 45,000	45,000	
P & L account 101,250	53,250	
Reserves brought forward 53,250		
	199,500	98,250

The net worth of the business at the end of 1993 is £98,250, rising to £199,500 at the end of 1994. On the basis that capital employed equals net worth plus long-term loans plus short-term loans, capital employed at 31 December 1993 = £173,250 and at 31 December 1994 = £244,500. Total assets at 31 December 1993 = £266,000 and at 31 December 1994 = £383,000. At the end of 1994, there is £73,000 in cash available, but total working capital of £129,500 (i.e. current assets –current liabilities).

Katie's Kitchens: Cash flow statement

For the year ending 31 December 1994

Cash flow statement		Explanations		Gross	VAT	Net
Receipts				Gross	VAT	Net
Cash		b/down	150,000	22,340	127,660	
Debtors	1,074,469	c/forward	(180,000)	(26,809)	(153,191)	
VAT	188,031	sales		192,500	1,100,000	
Loans	ˮ			188,031	1,074,469	
Other						
Total	1,262,500					
Stock movements						
Opening stock	25,000					
Purchases	570,000					
Usage	(550,000)			Gross	VAT	Net
Closing stock	45,000	b/down	50,000	7,447	42,553	
		c/forward	(64,750)	(9,644)	(55,106)	
Payments		purchases		99,750	570,000	
Trade creditors	557,447			97,553	557,447	
Wages	240,000					
Overhead costs	119,000	purchases		97,553		
Capital equipment	3,216	overheads		20,825	119,000	
Premises purchase	36,784	capital		7,000	40,000	
Loan repayments	30,000			125,378		
Loan interest	25,000					
Corporation tax	17,750	b/down		25,000		
VAT	125,378	c/forward		(20,000)		
VAT to C & E	69,925	sales		192,500		
Total	1,224,500	purchases		(99,750)		
Opening bank balance	35,000	overheads		(20,825)		
Movement for period	38,000	capital		(7,000)		
Closing bank balance	73,000	paid C&E		69,925		

Chapter 4

Katie's Kitchens: Profitability

$$Gross\ profit\ margin = \frac{550,000}{1,100,000} = 50\%$$

$$Net\ profit\ margin = \frac{180,000}{1,100,000} = 16\%$$

Excluding short-term bank lending

$$RoCE = \frac{180,000}{(199,500 + 15,000 + 98,250 + 45,000)/2} = 100\%$$

I prefer to include short-term bank lending, in which case

$$RoCE = \frac{180,000}{(199,500 + 15,000 + 30,000 + 98,250 + 45,000 + 30,000)/2} = 86\%$$

Remember that you should use the average for the period so add relevant figures from the opening and closing balance sheets and divide by 2.

$$RoE = \frac{(180,000 - 25,000 - 38,750)}{(199,500 + 98,250)/2} = \frac{116,250}{148,875} = 78\%$$

Katie's Kitchens: Solvency

$$Gearing = \frac{45,000}{244,500} = 18\%$$

$$Interest\ cover = \frac{180,000}{25,000} = 7$$

Katie's Kitchens: Liquidity

$$Current\ ratio = \frac{298,000}{165,500} = 1.8$$

$$Quick\ ratio = \frac{253,000}{168,500} = 1.5$$

Daily operating expenses can best be taken from the cash flow statement, so

$$Defensive\ interval = \frac{253,000}{1,224,500/365} = \frac{253,000}{3,355} = 75\ days$$

Katie's Kitchens: Efficiency

$$\text{Debtors' turnover ratio, d} = \frac{1,100,000}{(180,000 + 150,000)/2} = \frac{1,100,000}{165,000} = 6.7$$

$$\text{Average collection period} = \frac{365 \times (180,000 + 150,000)/2}{1,100,000} = 55 \text{ days}$$

$$\text{Creditors' turnover ratio, c} = \frac{550,000}{(64,750 + 50,000)/2} = \frac{550,000}{57,375} = 9.6$$

$$\text{Average payment period} = \frac{365 \times (64,750 + 50,000)/2}{550,000} = 38 \text{ days}$$

$$\text{Stock turnover ratio} = \frac{550,000}{(25,000 + 45,000)/2} = \frac{550,000}{35,000} = 15.7$$

$$\text{Average holding period} = \frac{365 \times (25,000 + 45,000)/2}{550,000} = 23 \text{ days}$$

$$\text{Asset turnover ratio} = \frac{1,100,000}{(298,000 + 85,000 + 210,000 + 56,000)/2} = \frac{1,100,000}{324,500} = 3.4$$

Chapter 5

Decor by Diane: Costing and pricing

The total costs are:

Five staff @ £15,000	£75,000
Overhead	£24,000
Drawings	£20,000
Your drawings are net, so you need to allow for tax	£7,500
You should allow a profit margin for reinvestment after tax, say	£11,000
Total costs	£137,500

If there are 240 jobs p.a., then the price for an average job = 137,500/240=	£573
You will need to add VAT 17.5%	£100
Sales price	£673

Note that this does not include materials which will have to be added. If the materials are fairly standard, for example, paint, then you could include it as part of your total costs. If materials costs vary dramatically, then add it afterwards:

Katie's Kitchens: Costing and Break even

There are two ways that we can approach the question of break even.

Firstly we can do it graphically. We know that Katie's fixed costs are over-heads plus interest giving a total of £395,000. (You must include depreciation because you need to recover that cost also). Total direct costs are £550,000. If Katie makes 2,000 units this gives total costs of £945,000. She forecasts that she can sell her 2,000 units at £550 each giving total income of £1,100,000. These figures can now be plotted on a break-even chart as shown below. From this, it can be seen that the break-even point is around 1,450 giving a margin of safety of around 550. (A larger graph will give a more accurate figure!).

Katie's Kitchens: Breakeven chart

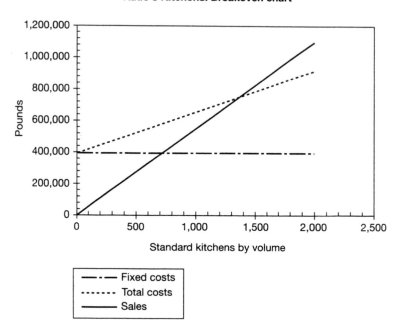

Katie could also do the calculation directly from the equation. For 2,000 units, the direct costs equal £275 per unit.

$$BE = \frac{370,000 + 25,000}{550 - 275} = 1,436$$

This gives a margin of safety of 564

The cost per standard kitchen is given by:

$$\frac{\text{Overheads and direct costs}}{\text{Total sales volume}} = \frac{395,000 + 550,000}{2,000} = £472.50$$

Colin's Cabinets

(a) Four drawers at 30 minutes gives 2 hours; adding 25 minutes for the shell, 30 minutes for painting and 5 minutes for final assembling and packing gives 3 hours.

(b) Efficiency ratio = standard hours/actual hours = 3/2.5 = 120 per cent

(c) You need to make a number of assumptions here. If everyone has 20 days' holiday and all their statutory holidays (8 days), each member of staff will expect to work 233 days of the year. Allowing an average, say, of 5 days' sick leave reduces this to 228 days. If everyone works 37.5 hours per week (i.e. 7.5 hours/day), the total hours available are 228 x 7.5 x 5= 8,550 hours p.a., equivalent to an average of 164.4 hours per week. This is the number of standard hours on which you base your budget.

(d) The capacity ratio=actual hours available/budgeted hours = 130/164.4 = 79 per cent.

Chapter 6

Eric's Engineering

You need to calculate the net present value for each option. Use a discount rate of 10 per cent.

	Year	*Cashflow*	*Discount Factor*	*Present Value*
Lathe	0	(20,000)	1.0000	(20,000)
	1	9,000	0.9091	8,181
	2	9,000	0.8264	7,434
	3	9,000	0.7513	6,759
	4	9,000	0.6830	6,147
	Net present value			8,521
Mill	0	(25,000)	1.0000	(25,000)
	1	7,000	0.9091	6,363
	2	7,000	0.8264	5,782
	3	7,000	0.7513	5,257
	4	7,000	0.6830	4,781
	5	7,000	0.6209	4,347
	6	7,000	0.5645	3,955
	Net present value			9,440

Both options give a positive NPV so Eric will get a better return by investing in a new machine compared to leaving his money in the bank. The milling machine gives a slightly better return so he should choose that option, if he can only afford one. On the other hand, he may be able to invest £5,000 in a different machine which may give a greater return than the difference between the mill and the lathe.

Chapter 9

Decor by Diane: Variances

1 Expected revenue is 20 jobs x £573 = £11,460. Actual sales have exceeded expected sales, but you cannot really answer the question until you have looked more carefully at how the figures are derived.

2 Labour variance and materials variance.

3 Let us look at the figures in more detail:

	Actual	Budget	Variance
Sales	13,000	13,100	100
less: materials	1,540	1,740	(200)
	11,460	11,360	(100)
Overheads			
Staff	6,250	7,000	(750)
Overheads	2,000	2,000	0
Net profit (including drawings etc)	3,210	2,360	(850)
less: drawings + tax	2,293	2,293	0
Retained earnings	917	67	(850)

Sales were higher than expected by £100, but this is more than cancelled out by the increased costs of £950. The business still has retained earnings which are positive but instead of 7 per cent of sales, retained earnings has fallen to just 0.5 per cent. While this is not disastrous, it might present difficulties if, for example, there are monthly loan repayments exceeding £67.

Index

■

absorption costing **83**
accounting centres **24**
accruals 31, 33
acid test 54
added value 8, 180
appraising capital investments
   94
appropriation account **35**
asset turnover 58, 66, 179

balance sheet 29, **36, 169**
benefits 7, 15
book-keeping 126, **128**
break-even analysis **80**
budget 10, 19
budgeting **22**, 108

capital assets 101
capital employed 40
capital expenditure budget 114
capital investments 94
cash book 128, **131**
cash flow forecasts **114**
cash flow statement 29, **42, 165**
Centre for Interfirm
   Comparisons 63
collection period 57
computers 144
contribution 24, 31, 80, 164
cost 60, 71, **72**
cost leadership 19
cost of sales 31
credit references **176**
creditors 38, 166, **177**
current assets 38
current liabilities 38
current ratio 54
customers 18

debenture 102
debtors 38, 166, **175**
defensive interval 55
Deming, Edward 14
depreciation 33, 90
differentiation 19
direct costs 31
discounted cash flow **96**
discounting **96**
double entry **136**
Drucker, Peter 15, 19

economic order quantities **110**
efficiency 48, **56**, 127
equity 40, 101

factoring **119**
features 7, 15
financial statements **29**
fixed assets 38, 89
focus 19
forecasting 114

gearing 51, 53
gearing, effect of 52
General Electric 181
goodwill 38
gross profit 31, 48, 74, 106

IBM 181
industry averages **63**
industry norms 47
interest cover 53
internal rate of return 97, **99**
invoice discounting **119**

labour turnover **168**
labour variances 158

leverage 52
Levi Strauss 16
liquidity 10,48, **53**, 127,151

management information
  systems **153**
manufacturing ratios **86**
marginal costing **84**
mark up 74
market research 107
materials purchase budget **109**
materials variances **158**
mission 16

net assets 40
net finance 40
net present value **97**
net profit 31, 48
net worth 40

objectives 17, 19, **20**
operational objectives 20
operating statement **162**
opportunity cost 5
order book 175
over-trading 8
overhead variances **160**
overheads 74, 161

payment period 57
payroll 141
petty cash **143**
plan, do, check, act 14
planning 15, **105**
Porter, Michael 15, 18
price elasticity **77**
pricing **71**
production budget **108**
production cost budget 114
profit **5**, 10
profit and loss account 29, **30**
profitability **48**, 127

purchase ledger **133**
purpose 6, 16

quick ratio 54

ratio tree 61
ratios 105
reconciliation 132, 148
records 11, 125, **126**
reducing balance depreciation **92**
return on capital 49, **95**, 105
risk assessment **103**

Sage Group 4, 142, 146, 168
sales budget **108**
sales ledger **133**
sales variances **156**
sensitivity analysis **120**
solvency 10, 48, **51**, 127
spreadsheets **170**
staff performance **62**, 64, 180
standard costing **85**
statutory requirements 127
stock control 110, **139**, 167, 179
stock holding period 57
straight line depreciation **91**
strategic objectives 66

total assets 49

value added analysis **64**
values 6
variance analysis **155**
VAT 31, 128, **149**
vision 14

wages book   141
work in progress 109
working capital 39, **117**
working capital cycle **8**

Young & Co's Brewery 32